CW01003896

A Taste of Murder

by Barrie Roberts

QuercuS

****

QuercuS

John Roberts

67, Cliffe Way, Warwick

CV34 5JG   01926 776363

john@walkwaysquercus.co.uk

www.walkwaysquercus.co.uk

****

A Taste of Murder

by Barrie Roberts

© Barrie Roberts

ISBN 1 898136 23 8

First Published 2004

Contents

NB The names of the places where the crime took place are followed by the county they were in at the time. This explains, for example, why a murder in Bilston was tried at the Stafford Assize, the county town. The oddity is "A damned sight better...", where part of Dudley, a Worcestershire town, was then in Staffordshire.

The Author

BARRIE ROBERTS was born in Hampshire in 1939 but has lived in the Midlands for over thirty years. For most of that time he worked in criminal law for two firms of solicitors, working on a number of murder cases, major frauds and the appeals of the Birmingham Six.

He is now a lecturer and writer whose books have been translated into Latvian, Malay, Russian and even American. They include *Sherlock Holmes and the Railway Maniac* (1994), *Sherlock Holmes and the Devil's Grail* (1996), *Sherlock Holmes and the Man from Hell* (1997), *Sherlock Holmes and the Royal Flush* (1998) and *Sherlock Holmes and the Harvest of Death* (1999). He has added four modern mystery novels: *The Victory Snapshot* (1998), *Robbery With Malice* (1999), *Bad Penny Blues* (2000) and *Crowner & Justice* (2002). He was the coauthor with Anne Bradford of three QuercuS books: *Midland Ghosts and Hauntings* (1994), *Midland Spirits and Spectres* (1997) and *Strange Meetings* (2002), and by himself wrote *Midland Murders & Mysteries* and *Murder in the Midlands*.

Barrie lectures for the City of Birmingham, teaching a long running course at Great Barr on Ghosts and Unsolved Mysteries. Apart from his professional involvement with the law, Barrie is a lifelong collector of accounts of crime cases and these cases come largely from his huge private library.

Sources and Acknowledgements

There is a vast number books and cuttings about past murders in my own library. However, for people who cannot spare forty years to make such a collection, let me name some other sources I have used in this book.

No writer on murder can ever ignore the work of those who have gone before and I must acknowledge much help from Michael Posner's *Midland Murders* (Star Publications, 1973), Betty Smith's *Warwickshire Murders* (Countryside Books, 1991), W.M.Jamieson's *Murders, Myths and Monuments of North Staffordshire* (Westmid Supplies, 1979) and Brian Lane's *The Murder Club Guide to the Midlands* (Harrap, 1988). In all of them you will find Midland cases which I have not included.

You can't research the past of the West Midlands without looking over the thirty years' of issues of the *Black Country Bugle*. This local magazine printed in the style of a Victorian popular newspaper hunts untiringly for stories of old crimes in its area, as well as ghosts and myths, and readers often supply personal memories and old documents.

Then there are the Public Libraries of the Midlands. I can't list them all but I must mention Birmingham Reference Library and the Salt Library at Stafford. I refer you also to the West Midlands Police Museum at Sparkbrook, Birmingham.

Where a Midland murder has attracted national attention I have sometimes turned to the *Notable British Trials* series and to the Penguin *Famous Trials*. For this book I also looked up Richard Harrison's *Criminal Calendar*, and his *Foul Deeds Will Rise*, as well as Joseph Wambaugh's *The Blooding* and Jack Smith-Hughes's *Unfair Comment* and *Six Studies in Villainy*.

Readers sometimes contact me with information, and I must thank Alan Baggott of Canberra, Australia, for information about the unsolved murder of Esther Baggott. Finally, I must thank my brother, the military historian Philip Roberts, for his help with the story of Captain John Donellan.

Barrie Roberts
2003

A Taste of Murder

Alfred, Lord Tennyson, after a long night chatting to a friend, added that only once before had he stayed up so late talking. It had been with Jowett, the philosopher. What had they talked about, his friend asked. "Murders", said the poet.

This story should convince those of you who share my taste for a good murder that we are not lone eccentrics. A great many people feel the same, and very few of them are ever likely to practice what they read.

Television transmits hours of murder each week, real and fictitious, newspapers are filled with the latest crimes, bookshops stuffed with true and invented murder stories, yet we live in a country that is the admiration and wonder of the world for its low murder rate. It seems that in Britain we don't treat murder as one of the fine arts, as De Quincy urged, but as entertainment rather than a DIY project. This is probably a very good thing.

Why are we so unmurderous? This question brings battalions of foreign criminologists, sociologists and psychiatrists to this strange little island but none of them seem sure of the answer. Is it because we have lived at peace and under some kind of rule of law for centuries longer than our neighbours, the USA or our former colonies? Is it relevant that we have not been invaded or occupied since 1066 nor suffered civil war since 1652?

Certainly, wars increase violent crime, when the lads are discharged and some apply their new skills to making a dishonest living or getting rid of people they don't like. Even so, soldiers have been returning from our wars, foreign and colonial, since the mid 1600s, probably more than any other country, yet one American city can match England's annual murder total. Even Canada (when did you last read of a famous Canadian murder?) has about four times our national rate.

All of which is very comforting. Less comforting is the fact that most British murders are committed by someone close to the victim, a relative, friend, spouse or colleague. Most of them are cleared up very quickly, for that reason, which makes the selection of truly interesting cases very difficult. I could fill shelf after shelf with books about spouses battered to death, stabbed or strangled in arguments, but they would make very dull reading.

As in my two previous books of murders in the western Midlands, I have tried to avoid that and to offer cases that have some genuine interest or peculiarity. So here is a country solicitor who was blackmailed twice and wouldn't put up with it, a man who died mysteriously at the hands of one of three possible killers and a stalker who was caught by an astonishing coincidence. Then there is the multiple murderer and kidnapper who was caught by a routine police patrol, the man who certainly killed once (maybe twice) but ended up murdered, a man who killed a total stranger and went to the gallows with an explanation that makes no sense. And you can read about the doctor who killed because of snobbery, the man who killed to avoid the workhouse and a coward who let two of his friends hang while he kept silent.

These cases range across the Midlands and across time, from the 17th to the 20th centuries. Most of them are more than a quarter of a century old, partly to avoid awakening recent grief or anger, partly because more recent cases are still remembered. There is one exception, a case from the 1980s which I have included because of its unique position in the history of crime detection. Once again, thank you to the people who suggested particular cases. In the note on sources you will find recommendations for further reading.

If you share the preoccupations of Jowett and Lord Tennyson, I hope this book will provide interest, entertainment and food for thought.

"Verily, a wicked deed was done."
(Alcester, Warks 1693)

There are places that seem designed for murder, places that give you the creeps in daylight, places that ooze an unwholesome, sickening atmosphere. One such was Moon's Moat which is now part of Redditch.

Three hundred years ago it was a dark and stagnant pool which already had a reputation as being haunted. Close by it stood the crumbling manor of the Moon family, a dynasty as decayed as their dwelling. In January 1693 the Moat House was occupied by Joan Moon, a widow, her three sons and their half-sister, Mariolle. They were rarely seen about and had a reputation as recluses.

Late on the bitter midwinter night of 14th January 1693, Richard Gale, the Beoley constable, found himself near the Moat House. He must have had a fire and comforts calling him home and cannot have wanted to linger in such a repellent place.

Suddenly the shriek of a woman stabbed across the still, black waters of Moon's Moat. Fearfully, Gale stopped and waited. A second terrible shriek convinced Gale that a woman was being seriously mistreated. He moved towards the Moat in time to see a body flung from an upper window of the Moat House. Then there was silence, no more shrieks, no movement at the window. The body splashed into the black pool and sank, then there was silence. Perhaps wisely, Richard Gale decided that whatever had just taken place, there was nothing to be done about it that night. He made his way home.

Gale returned next day with two colleagues and searched the Moat House. Nothing was found to show that anything was amiss, though Mariolle was missing. Her family said she was visiting London. A search of the Moat produced a woman's dark serge cloak, but no body. None of this convinced Gale. He stood by the evidence of his ears and eyes. "Verily", he said, "a wicked deed was done last night". Most likely he was right, for Mariolle Moon was never seen again.

The Moat House stood about eight miles from Alcester, and next day there arrived at the Angel Inn one Captain Richard Hill. A couple of letters, addressed to "Captain Richards" were already waiting for him. He was shown to one of the best rooms and settled in. Captain Hill was a good looking young man with an easy charm, and Alcester soon found that a dull provincial midwinter was relieved by this well spoken, witty and travelled guest.

Rural Alcester three centuries ago was probably not a social magnet to urbane characters like Captain Hill. What brought him to that backwater in the dead of winter? Why was his correspondence under a false name?

The sinister Moat today, an interesting feature in a pleasant little patch of woodland somewhere in the rolling suburbia of Redditch.

MOONS MOAT

The site of a medieval moated homestead dating from the 14th century. Rebuilding took place in the 16th century and the moat was recut to its present form. The site was finally abandoned in the 17th century.

A SCHEDULED ANCIENT MONUMENT

Quite simply, the witty Captain was wanted for murder. In December 1692 he was in London enjoying the company of a boon friend, Charles, Baron Mohun of Okehampton, who despite his title, was a sordid, drunken teenage ruffian. Baron and Captain passed their time in the capital drinking, playing cards and womanising.

The toast of London's young men at the time was Ann Bracegirdle, a lovely young actress then starring at the Drury Lane Theatre. When Mohun and Hill set their eyes upon her they decided she should be theirs. That is, both of them wanted her but their friendship meant that they were prepared to share her favours.

Ann Bracegirdle put off their advances, probably not only because she was in love with William Mountford, a fellow Drury Lane actor. Mountford lived (with his wife, it should be said) in Norfolk Street, while Ann lived with her mother in the connected Howard Street, close to the Strand.

On 9th December 1692 the frustrated admirers, Mohun and Hill, decided to take matters into their own hands. With a coach and a pair of hired thugs they set off to Drury Lane only to find that Ann Bracegirdle was not appearing that night.

They went on to the lady's house where they were told that she and her mother were dining with friends, the Pages, in Drury Lane. It was still early for a dinner party to end, so Mohun and Hill took advantage of several inns on their way, arriving back in Drury Lane well drunk. Then they waited in the street until about 10 o'clock when Mrs Bracegirdle and her daughter emerged from their friends' house.

Mohun and Hill grabbed Ann and tried to bundle her into the coach. Like many wooers, though, they had reckoned without the lady's mother. Mrs Bracegirdle took hold of her daughter and set up such a noise as threatened to bring the whole city. Certainly it frightened away the hired thugs and brought some help. Mohun and Hill were sent about their business and the ladies were escorted safely home.

The frustrated kidnappers restored themselves in another tavern and some time later returned to Ann Bracegirdle's house even more drunk. Now they pleaded that they wished to apologise and explain their actions. She refused to see them, so they prowled outside, making a lot of noise and uttering bloodcurdling threats against poor William Mountford who had played no part in the evening's coarse melodrama.

The actress became concerned for Mountford's safety and sent a message to his home urging him to stay out of sight. The message never reached him. Walking home from the theatre he arrived near Ann's home where he was spotted by the drunken Mohun and Hill.

They seized the actor and demanded to know about his relations with Ann Bracegirdle. He told them that she was "no concern of mine". Hill drew his sword and Mountford said to Mohun, "I hope your Lordship will not countenance any ill action on the part of Mr Hill".

Hill struck Mountford about the head and Mountford cried out, "Damme! What's all this?" It was the last line he ever delivered. Mohun held the actor while Hill ran him through with his sword several times. Dropping the body to the cobbles, the two ruffians ran off.

Mohun was soon caught and, as a Baron, was entitled to be tried by "a jury of his peers" that is, in the House of Lords. That thoughtful body might have considered Mohun's youth or the fact that he was a member of the most exclusive club in the world. At all events, they decided that although Mohun had held Mountford while Hill stabbed him, Hill had been the actual killer, so they acquitted the mad Baron. Be warned, this decison is not to be treated as a precedent. It was bad law then and it is bad law now. If you hold someone while a friend murders them you will be charged and convicted as a murderer.

✵✵✵✵✵✵✵

Mohun's trial and acquittal were held on 31st January. By then Captain Hill was long gone. It seems that before he reached the Angel, Alcester, he was a guest at the crumbling home of the Moon's, Moat House. This was an excellent hideaway since visitors were few and the Moons never socialised.

His move to the Angel changed his social status. He became a sought after guest at parties around Alcester. Winter was well under way and the Christmas festivities must have exhausted local social resources. A new face in the town was a blessing. London was distant, nobody travelled in winter without a vital reason and there were no illustrated papers, radio or television to carry his picture.

Captain Richard Hill settled down to enjoy the pleasures of country living and did so with great success until the night of the Pumphreys' party. This important local family invited Hill to an event at their home near Alcester Town Hall. There he danced with a local beauty, Miss Moll Pratley, after which he settled to play cards with the gentlemen.

What started the trouble has been forgotten. Whether Hill spoke out of turn about his dancing partner or whether he was seen cheating is forgotten. What followed was an argument which heated up to the point where Hill drew his sword. Rural Warwickshire life may have been dull, but it did not require to be livened by swordplay. He was quickly overpowered and thrown out, swearing his vengeance on those who had humiliated him.

Next morning dramatic versions of the card room confrontation of Hill's angry threats must have excited all Alcester and beyond, but they were soon overtaken by other news. Far from setting out on the trail of revenge, Captain Hill seems to have packed his box and left Alcester early in the morning. Few would have been sorry to see him go and no one seems to have wondered or worried when they never heard of him again.

****

Nearly a century and a half passed. The Angel carried on serving travellers, though it developed a reputation as haunted. Bumps and bangs were heard at night but this did not prevent the young Princess Victoria sleeping there in 1832.

In 1837 the Angel closed to become a private house and during conversion a discovery was made. Tucked into an old, bricked-up oven the builders found a travelling box. It contained a warm travelling cloak, a low crowned felt hat, several ornamental buckles, a snuff box and a fancy waistcoat ornamented with gold thread. There were also two rusting swords and a pair of letters, both addressed to Captain Richard Hill, one in English and one in French and both about loans.

So Captain Hill, if he had left the Angel, had gone without his travelling chest, swords or cloak. If he had not paid his bill why did Miss Hancock (who ran the Angel) not sell his belongings to cover the debt? Why were they walled up in an oven? Did somebody else settle Richard Hill's affairs in every way?

It is certain that Hill killed Mountjoy in London. It is probable that he killed Mariolle Moon in Beoley. Was he killed himself by his old enemies from London catching up with him, by the Moons seeking to eliminate a dangerous witness, by an admirer of Moll Pratley, by some outraged cardplayer? We shall never know who did it but it seems safe to say that Captain Hill was murdered at the Angel.

[Captain Hill has appeared in another QuercuS book – *Midland Ghosts & Hauntings* in a story named "The Mocking Laugh of Captain Richard Hill". So now you have the gallant captain both living and dead.]

"Like a bag of blood"
(Birmingham, 1931)

When America sneezes, they say, Britain catches a cold. We certainly catch a lot of things from America. Columbus brought back gold and syphilis, Raleigh gave us potatoes and tobacco, then there are zip fasteners and safety razors, ragtime and jazz, talking pictures and gramophones, chewing gum and peanut butter, cars with tail fins, rock'n roll, country music, serial killers and fast food.

Perhaps the most effective infection was the sound movies because they showed us all the other delights of American life and helped us to imitate them. The nastiest was probably in 1929 when America suffered the Wall Street Crash, an infectious financial condition that turned into the worldwide Great Depression.

****

By the summer of 1931 that financial flu had taken a firm hold in Britain. The West Midlands was deeply dependent on manufacturing industry and jobs were disappearing. Two young men out of work that summer were Herbert Ridley and Victor Betts. Both lived near Six Ways, Aston in Birmingham and both were 21. Ridley was married and had been a van driver but he had been out of work for months when he met Betts in the dole queue. Ridley's concern was to find cash to keep his family; Betts, formerly a blacksmith, had other priorities. An habitual cinema goer, he admired the American gangster style and imitated it when he could afford to with sharply cut suits and snappy hats.

Betts resented his position and sought ways to raise cash. He tried one method with a pal called Charlie Ludwyche when they attacked a motor dealer called Al Chalmers who was said to carry a wallet stuffed with notes. The rumour was wrong and they netted only three pounds. Betts was so angry that he beat Chalmers with a broken chairleg. Ludwyche was disappointed at the low profit and very disturbed by his partner's violence, so decided that a life of crime was not for him. Betts branded him a coward and uttered severe threats about leaking any information.

Victor Betts soon had another criminal prospect in mind, but he needed a partner and a car. His new chum Bert Ridley could drive and had let Betts know that he was willing to try anything to raise money.

Betts had learned from a girl at a dance that she worked for W M Taylor (Drapers) Ltd, whose shop was in Potters Hill, Aston. Every weekday morning, she told him, an elderly messenger from Taylor's carried a bag of the previous day's takings some 500 yards along the street to the National Provincial Bank's branch at Six Ways, Aston. The bag, she said, contained hundreds of pounds every day.

Victor Betts chewed over the information and checked it by watching the messenger on about half a dozen occasions. The carrier of the bag was a small man in his 60's with a limp who was meticulous about timing, never varying his routine by more than a minute or two.

Armed with his knowledge of American gangster movies, Betts created a plot and broached it to Bert Ridley when they met at Aston Labour Exchange. Ridley didn't take much convincing.

On the morning of 21st July the two bandits synchronised their watches, as all the best movie robbers do, then Ridley went to a garage and paid 5 shillings [25p] to hire a car. If Betts had been the planner that he thought he was he would have warned Ridley to pick an unexceptional vehicle. As it was, Ridley chose a bright yellow saloon.

He parked the car in Rifle Street where he sat with the engine idling as he waited for the appointed time. As zero hour neared he moved the car slowly to the junction in time to see Betts, muffler round his face and hat pulled well down, walk along the street and catch up with an old man carrying a leather bag.

The small, elderly messenger was William Andrews, then aged 62. He had worked for Taylor's since his boyhood and it was forty years since Mr Taylor had appointed him to carry the bank bag. Walking his familiar route on that sunny July morning, he must have felt well satisfied that he had a secure job at his age while younger men were on the dole. Within seconds events proved that he would have been better out of work.

As Victor Betts came up with Andrews he struck a vicious blow to the old man's head and snatched the leather bag. The elderly messenger crumpled to the pavement, Ridley slowed alongside and Betts leapt aboard. A moment later the yellow car roared off.

There was little traffic and few people on the street, but Charles Dowd in his open touring car had seen the attack and chased the yellow car. Ridley was a native of north Birmingham and, knowing the side streets, he dodged, turned and zig-zagged through the slums until they had shaken off their pursuer. Then they headed for Claverdon Street where Betts had booked them a place in a cheap lodging house.

Safe inside for the time being, they examined their haul. Betts slit the locked bag and out tumbled no less than £905/5sh/2d [£905.26p], the equivalent in today's money of many thousands.

Delighted with their success, the two quickly left Claverdon Street and made for another lodging house in Windsor Street. There they washed and relaxed, split the cash and decided it was time to leave Birmingham. They were soon on a northbound train.

They were comfortably settled in a Leeds hotel and beginning to enjoy the fruits of their crime when they saw a newspaper story that William Andrews had died from Betts's blow. Now they were not just successful robbers but wanted murderers. Quickly they packed, changed direction again and made for Brighton.

As the hot summer days passed the two feckless killers sampled the pleasures of the sunny South Coast resorts. They met two young Bristol women on holiday in Brighton and as a foursome they toured together in expensive hired cars. Betts told his girl, Beattie Stone, that he had wealthy parents who had given him £500 for his holiday, and he presented her with a £20 diamond ring. Ridley made out that he was a professional footballer with Aston Villa being well paid in the off season. One day they found themselves near Chichester where Betts decided it was his turn to drive. He crashed the car and all four ended up overnight in the Royal East Sussex Hospital. Still, they were all discharged in the morning and the holiday went on, costing nearly £40 pounds a day.

Meanwhile, back in Birmingham, Chief Superintendent Burnett was piecing together clues that he hoped would trap the killers. The post mortem on their victim showed that he had been killed by a violent blow to the left side of his head, probably with a blunt object. The leather bag was found and identified at the Claverdon Street lodging house where the landlady gave a good description of her two short term lodgers. Charles Dowd who had chased the yellow car also described the killers. The girl who had talked out of turn to Betts admitted her stupid mistake to her workmates and was interviewed by the police. Her statement took them to Victor Betts's lodgings, where they heard that he had been absent since the morning of 21st July. A check at Aston Labour Exchange confirmed that Betts had drawn no dole since the killing, and neither had his pal Ridley.

Burnett got hold of photographs of both men and circulated their pictures across Britain.

******

Seaside resorts in summer draw villains from all over the country, mingling with the holidaymaker in the cause of more crime or simply taking a holiday. The police in these resorts know that the summer means watching for other people's criminals as well as their own. As Herbert Ridley strolled on Brighton's Grand Parade in the August sunshine, Inspector Wells of Brighton Police recognised a face from a poster. Taking Ridley's arm, he arrested him on suspicion of murder.

At Brighton Police Station Ridley soon gave in and then Betts was arrested. The police recovered less than £250 of the stolen money. It had been an expensive fortnight in Brighton. Ridley told the police that he wanted to get rid of the money that they had killed for; "It was like a bag of blood in my pocket".

Chief Superintendent Burnett, Chief Inspector Bagley and Inspector Dillon travelled to Brighton to bring the two prisoners back to Birmingham where they were both charged with the murder of William Andrews. On 4th December 1931 they were tried at Birmingham Assize and on the following day the jury took a surprising hour to find them both guilty. The judge sentenced them to hang.

Betts took his sentence calmly but Ridley turned pale and staggered in the dock. Both lodged appeals which were heard on 19th December. In the view of the Court of Appeal there was no reason to interfere with the jury's verdict, but Mr Justice Avory added a comment that, "there might be a distinction to be drawn by those who had the duty, which this Court has not, of considering the sentence".

The public often sympathises with those who kill in passion or fear, but rarely with those who kill entirely for profit. Nevertheless, there was a groundswell of public opinion in favour of Ridley who had not struck the murderous blow. Mr Justice Avory's words were a clear indication to the Home Secretary that the Appeal Judges felt the same.

Victor Betts career as a sharp gangster ended on the gallows at Winson Green Prison. Herbert Ridley was gaoled for life.

"Someone up there
who knows the truth'
(Walsall, Staffs 1970)

Early in the summer of 1970 as Britain prepared for a General Election, the West Midlands had a heatwave.

One hot Sunday evening that June, in Rowley Street, Walsall, Joyce Smith put her two children to bed and entertained a neighbour for a while. Rowley Street is a quiet residential street off Walsall's ring road and close to the town's beautiful Arboretum. It had seen many of its big houses divided into flats or turned into boarding houses.

In the early months of 1970 the usual calm had been disturbed by a character who became known as the Rowley Street Rapist. After dark he accosted lone women in the walled footpath that led to one end of the street or in the access alleys and pathways around their homes. At night he hung about houses where there were unprotected women.

Joyce Smith was a handsome West Indian woman with a failed marriage behind her who was both a conductor on Walsall Corporation buses and the landlady of Number 70. Here she lived with her cousin, Clifton Blair, her children, and a lodger called Isaac Scott.

There had been another lodger, a lady whom I shall call Clarice, but she had left the house a few weeks before, suddenly and secretly.

As Joyce chatted to her neighbour she prepared a meal but did not eat it, saying that she might wait and see if her boyfriend called later in the evening and eat with him. The neighbour left at about 9.30 and became the last person but one to see Joyce Smith alive.

Joyce's cousin Clifton was a bus driver in his late 30s. He was a skilful cricketer and he had passed that summer Sunday playing with the Aldridge team. After the match he returned to the clubhouse in Aldridge and when the club closed accepted a lift home from a team mate. He was dropped off on the Broadway a short distance from Rowley Street and walked to his home, arriving at about 11 o'clock.

The house was in darkness and Joyce apparently in bed. Clifton was tired from his day's sport and had an early shift in the morning. He went to bed and slept for a short while before hearing the front door of the house open. He thought it was Isaac Scott, Scotty, coming home and got up to ask Scotty for a match so that Clifton could brew a coffee before going out in the morning.

Scotty was a hairdresser specialising in the hair of West Indians who tend to think that white barbers don't understand it. He had spent much of the evening in a business discussion with a successful West Indian hairdresser in the town, putting a proposal that she should take him into partnership. He was told that he needed more than his skill to make him a partner, that he would have to bring in money or equipment. He had neither, so the proposal failed. Later he visited friends before returning to Rowley Street.

✷✷✷✷✷✷✷

Early on Monday morning Clifton Blair got up, made himself coffee and went off to work. Shortly after, at about 7.15, Scotty got up and went to knock on Joyce Smith's door. He said afterwards that he thought she might have overslept and missed her shift. Getting no answer he entered the room. She lay dead in her bed, struck with one ferocious punch and then strangled.

It was evident that the killer was male because he had ejaculated all over the bedding so the three men closest to Joyce were rapidly investigated. Her ex-husband was able to show an unshakable alibi and her boyfriend established that he had spent the night with another woman in Wolverhampton. Clifton Blair was taken to Walsall Police Station for questioning, held for several hours, then released. DNA testing had not been discovered and grouping of the semen stains on Joyce's bed merely established that the strangler was not her boyfriend.

Scotland Yard was called in, as usual in those days, and Superintendent Barnett arrived. He was later chief of the Met.'s Drug Squad and after retirement, a crime novelist. The General Election came as detectives mingled with canvassers around Rowley Street. Hundreds of witnesses were interviewed but no lead appeared. Clifton Blair was questioned again at his solicitor's office. After a fortnight Barnett returned to London, the press reporting that he had gone to consult an expert.

On the Saturday morning after Barnett's return to Walsall police officers called at the Rowley Street boarding house where Blair had been staying since the crime. He was arrested and charged with murder.

A Case to Answer

Before a serious criminal case can be tried a Magistrate's Court must decide that there is a case to answer. When the prosecution evidence was released to Blair's solicitors it was evident that the case hinged on one factor only, a calculation of the time at which Joyce Smith had died.

Television plays and thriller novels are full of police doctors who examine a body briefly and announce that, "He died between midnight and one in the morning". It is never that easy. The fixing of time of death is the most difficult exercise for forensic pathologists and wide margins have to be set.

Joyce Smith had been found dead at about 7.15 am. Police doctor Lester had arrived soon after but did not take a temperature reading at the scene. The body was eventually moved from the bedroom, placed in a van and taken to the morgue where, at about noon a temperature was taken.

Superintendent Barnett had taken the report of Dr Hewspear, the Walsall pathologist who carried out the post mortem, to Professor Keith Simpson, who had calculated a narrowly limited time of death. Simpson pointed out that in strangulation cases the body temperature rises sharply just before death.

In this case he estimated it could have risen to as much as 105 degrees. Immediately after death a body begins to cool, and the figure normally applied was 1.5 degrees of cooling per hour. Joyce Smith was partly clothed and covered by bedclothes, in a closed room on a hot June night. In those circumstances Simpson suggested that a rate of .5 degrees per hour was more likely. Taking the temperature found by Dr Hewspear at noon, Simpson deducted it from 105 degrees and divided the result by .5 degrees. The result was 12.5 hours, putting the time of death close to 11.30 pm, a time when, according to his own evidence and that of Scotty, Clifton Blair was the only adult male in the house.

The Trial

The case was committed for trial at Stafford Assizes and then Dr Hewspear fell ill. The defence was asked if they wanted the trial delayed so that Hewspear could attend, or could his evidence be read to the Jury? Dr Hewspear's findings appeared to be irrelevant. What mattered was the calculation which Simpson had based upon them, so the case went ahead.

The trial began in Stafford's old Shire Hall in November 1970. Trying to establish a motive, the Crown called a witness who visited number 70 Rowley Street and saw Clifton and Joyce engaged in bawdy horseplay, apparently to show that he had a powerful lust for his cousin. They put forward a scientist who had examined fabric threads found under Joyce's fingernails who said that they showed "close agreement" with samples taken from a dressing gown owned by Blair. They pointed to semen stains on the underwear Blair wore when arrested, as though the idea of semen stains on the underpants of a single man was the most extraordinary thing in the world. The arresting officers gave evidence that, shortly after his arrest, Blair had said "I keep seeing her lying there". He had not seen her lying dead unless he had killed her, they argued.

Most of this was irrelevant. Nobody had evidence that Blair and Joyce Smith had a sexual relationship. The textile fragments did not match Blair's dressing gown. Mr Simmens, of the Shirley Institute, Britain's most prestigious textile laboratory, identified them as coming from a Walsall Corporation Transport uniform, and it seems likely that they lodged behind the fingernails when Joyce put out her uniform on Sunday night, most particularly when she slid her shift timetable into the breast pocket. Blair had seen Joyce Smith at the mortuary, so he had seen her, "lying there".

The crux of the case remained Professor Simpson's calculation of the time of death, and this meant that the defence had a problem.

Those of you who have sat on committees will know that when the Treasurer presents his report many people pay no attention, convinced that they cannot understand figures. Juries behave in the same way over scientific evidence. Believing that they do not understand science they allow expert evidence to flow past their ears without trying to follow it.

To get across to the jury the extremely slender basis of Professor Simpson's calculation, Douglas Draycott QC, leading for the defence, was painstaking in cross examining the pathologist. Step by step he led the Professor through the estimates, opinions and guesses that formed the planks of his structure. Each time, Simpson justified them on the basis that he thought that was correct.

"Let me put it this way" began Draycott, asking his last question, "here you have an approximate body..." and went on to set out the chain of estimate, opinion and guess which led to the time of death. The Professor missed the irony. "I could not", he confirmed, "have put it better myself".

The Jury missed the irony as well. They returned a guilty verdict and Blair was sentenced to life imprisonment. As he was sentenced he pointed a dramatic finger at the high public gallery of the old courtroom and declared, "There is someone up there who knows the truth".

First Appeal

The defence applied for leave to appeal. Dr Hewspear had recovered from his illness and was asked by the prosecution to review his report before the hearing. He realized that there were two serious errors in the typed text of the document. Firstly, two sentences had been garbled and run together, secondly, a figure had been mis-typed. The mangled sentences had been where he reported that the temperature taken at the morgue might not be a useful guide to the time of death, and by an astounding coincidence the inaccurate figure was the temperature itself, where an error of one degree had been made. Leave to appeal was granted and the court decided that the case must be retried.

The Courts Act which abolished Quarter Sessions and Assizes had come into force while the appeal was dealt with, so that the retrial took place in the newly created Birmingham Crown Court.

There was little that was new in the fresh hearing. Although discredited at Stafford, the Crown again called the evidence about textile fragments. They were bound to recall Professor Simpson and, equally inevitably, the defence suggested to him that an alteration of one degree in the temperature of the corpse made, according to his theories, a difference of two hours, putting the death well into the small hours of the morning, when Isaac Scott was in the house.

Simpson would have none of it. He insisted that at the first trial he had said that he based his timing on three factors, the state of digestion, the state of rigor mortis and the temperature. They had all shown close agreement. The error of one degree did not, he insisted, make a difference of two hours. Taken with the other two factors, it merely pushed the time on a bit, perhaps nearer to midnight.

There was a problem with this argument. The stomach contents can be examined and will give a rough time when death stopped digestion, if you know when the meal was eaten. Nobody could say when Joyce ate her supper. Her neighbour said that it was ready but not eaten when she left at 9.30. It might have been eaten at any time after that.

Rigor mortis is a notoriously unreliable guide to time of death. Usually it starts to set in immediately after death, spreads through all the limbs, then starts to pass off, taking as long as it took to set in. Even so, it is sometimes faster and sometimes slower and sometimes does not occur at all. Added to which there was no reliable account of the state of rigor in Joyce Smith's body. Dr Lester did not note it and the lay witnesses' comments were confusing.

Fence and fudge as he might, Professor Simpson had painted himself into a corner with his half a degree an hour calculation. The alteration in Hewspear's report made it much more likely that Joyce had died after 1 o'clock, rather than after 11 o'clock.

The defence called Simpson's great professional opponent, Professor Francis Camps. He was scornful of attempts to pin down time of death to minutes and suggested that a time after 1 o'clock was as near as could be suggested.

****

Clifton Blair had not given evidence at Stafford, persuaded by his lawyers that he had answered the police questions in full and had no reason to expose himself to cross-examination. Having been convicted he obviously believed that he should give evidence at Birmingham.

He was not a good witness, stressed and surly in the witness box, but there was worse. Asked to account for the semen stains on his underwear he said that he had been sexually involved with a married woman that weekend. He was asked her name and address and gave it.

The inevitable followed. The Crown called Mrs X (let's call her). She testified that she and Clifton had been lovers and she had become pregnant by him. The pregnancy forced her to reveal her adultery to her husband, who forgave her but made her swear never to see Clifton Blair again. She had not seen him for a long time at the date of the murder. Whether she was telling the truth or not, it seemed to brand him as a liar.

There was a further surprise. As Mrs X left the court there was a new arrival in the public gallery. Derval Bloomfield had been a frequent visitor to Number 70 and he recognised the last witness. He plunged into court and explained his information to the defence lawyers, who sought and obtained leave to call him as a late witness.

He said that days before the murder he had visited Number 70 during the day and had seen Mrs X there. He had not known who she was until afterwards, when Joyce Smith had told him that the lady was Clifton's girlfriend, so it seemed that she had continued to see him.

What the Jury made of all this we can't know and it is forbidden to ask. Unhappily, when a case gets complicated jurors tend to fall back on, "There's no smoke without fire", and convict. The Judge's summing up was hostile to the defendant, going so far as to invent theories which the prosecution had not put forward. For example, he suggested that there were no fragments of Blair's skin under Joyce's fingernails (a frequent finding in strangulation cases) because the textile fragments had prevented that. The textile fragments were dust sized. Whatever the reason, the jury convicted Clifton Blair again.

Second Appeal

His barristers thought that the game was at an end and that further appeal was pointless, but his solicitor, Walsall's Ivan Geffen, thought otherwise and lodged another appeal. Colin Coode, junior defence counsel, presented a vigorously argued application to the Court of Appeal and won at last agreement that the Crown had presented two different cases at the two different trials and that there should be a full hearing at which the Crown might, if it could, explain the situation.

The defence began to hope. Double jeopardy, or being tried twice for the same crime, can happen in Britain, but treble jeopardy, never. If the Court of Appeal accepted the defence arguments, Clifton Blair's conviction should quashed.

It was not to be. When the case came before the Court of Appeal the judges decided that they could not deal with the case. The appeal, they said, was from the conviction in the second trial; it was based on a comparison of the first and second trials. They could not look at any aspect of the first trial in dealing with an appeal from the second.

This was bad law. In 1968 the High Court had said that the Court of Appeal had a duty to consider not just the facts of a case, but all the surrounding circumstances. The fact that it had been tried twice was surely one of the facts surrounding it?

The real reason, I suspect, why the Court of Appeal would not touch the case was fear, fear that they would have to accept the appeal and set Blair free, since they could not order yet another retrial. If they did that the jackals of the tabloid press would be yelping that the Court of Appeal had set free a man twice convicted by juries of strangling. The Court was simply not prepared to face the bad publicity.

So Clifton Blair settled down to face a life sentence leaving unanswered the question of what really took place in Number 70 Rowley Street on that hot Sunday night.

Unanswered...

At the Stafford trial there had been mention of the Rowley Street Rapist and the fact that the back door of the house was always unlocked. Had the prowler found the house open and entered to let his fantasies explode into deadly violence? Before the second trial he had been caught, identified entering an off-licence by Eileen Adshead who had seen him face to face, and placed under citizen's arrest by Nick Withers, whose wife had been attacked by the prowler. He was convicted on charges of assault, but not it seems, questioned about the death of Joyce Smith.

Then there was Blair's dramatic declaration as he was sentenced. Was there someone in the public gallery who knew the truth? Blair believed that there was, a woman who knew that Scotty was the killer. Was that possible?

The evidence showed that the strangler was male. Leaving aside outsider possibilities like the Rowley Street Rapist, two men were known to have been in that house on the murder night. According to the Crown's first attempt it could only have been Blair because of the timing, but the corrected evidence in the second trial seemed to shift the time of death forward into the period when both men were at home.

The Crown never established a reasonable motive for Blair to kill his cousin. He and Joyce grew up together as children, and that tends to prevent later sexual interest. Nobody could give any evidence of a sexual relationship between them or of Blair's desire for his cousin. If Blair had no motive, did Scott have one?

"I did it for a reason."
(Uttoxeter, Staffs 1955)

Donald Haywood Lainton came from Stockport. He was 28 years old, married, and worked in insurance. It was his ill luck that on a chilly day in February 1955 business took him to Uttoxeter, Staffordshire,.

✱✱✱✱✱✱✱

Killers, robbers, burglars – the perpetrators of crimes can often be found by asking one question, "Who had the motive, means and opportunity to commit the crime?"

Motives are the thoughts, feelings and wishes which cause people to do things. In murder investigations they can be a great help to the police. The question, "Who did this thing?" is followed naturally by "Who benefits?", and very often the answer reveals the culprit.

Once a suspect has been charged, though, motive becomes far less important. English law does not require a prosecutor to show the motive for any crime. Prosecutors try to show what was done and who did it, but they tend to leave alone why it was done. Putting forward a theory about motive which the defence can disprove might seriously damage a prosecutor's case.

With murder there are not many motives, greed, lust, fear, hatred, vengeance just about cover the field, with insanity where none of them apply. Even where a suspect makes no confession, gives no evidence at his trial and remains silent afterwards, it is often possible to work out what moved him. Not always.

Whether Donald Lainton had completed his business by lunchtime we do not know. Maybe he just decided to take a break. Whatever the reason, he had a drink in a Uttoxeter pub where he met a 34 year old concrete moulder from Great Haywood called Frederick Arthur Cross. Pubs in the 1950s were much less likely to serve food than they are now, and when Lainton raised the question of lunch Cross told him that he knew where Lainton could get a meal. They left the pub together and went off in Lainton's car.

What happened next remains a mystery. At some point Cross must have suggested to Lainton that he turn the car into a drive. That is where it was later found. Lainton was still in it, unconscious and severely wounded. He was taken to Stafford General Infirmary but died without regaining consciousness. On 1ˢᵗ March Frederick Cross was charged with his murder.

Donald Lainton had ten stab wounds in his head and neck. Whatever happened in the parked car had been explosively violent and only one man could explain it, Frederick Cross.

If you are charged with murder in Britain there is little point in pleading guilty because the law prescribes only one sentence. Until 1964 it was hanging; now it is life imprisonment. Knowing what will happen if you plead guilty, no matter how poor your story or how convincing the Crown's evidence, it is always worth gaining a faint chance by pleading not guilty.

In 1955 we were still hanging convicted murderers and the public fully expected that Frederick Cross would take the usual route and plead not guilty, offering some kind of explanation for the violent death of Donald Lainton.

In July Cross appeared before Mr Justice Gorman at Stafford Assizes but when the charge was put to him he pleaded guilty. The Judge explained that legal assistance could be provided if Cross required it, "but I understand", he said, "that you have said that you do not want it".

The Judge's remarks were repeated slowly to Cross by the dock warder. "No", said Cross, "I want to plead guilty". Mr Justice Gorman took pains to make sure that the prisoner understood what he was doing. "You do understand, don't you", he asked, "that if you plead guilty to this charge I have no alternative but to pass the sentence? Do you fully understand that?"

Again the dock officer repeated the Judge's words. The prisoner answered, "Yes, sir" and was sentenced to hang. The Home Secretary reviewed the case but found no grounds for a reprieve. Frederick Cross was hanged at Winson Green Prison, Birmingham on 27th July 1955.

So, what was it all about? Cross did make a statement which seemed to be a confession to a weird kind of suicide:

> "My wife had left me on New Year's Day with another man: she didn't answer my letters. I brooded over this and made up my mind to do away with myself.....I am not worth being sorry for, but I am sorry for the man, and I wish I had known before I did this that he was married....I don't want to live, I have nothing to live for."

Suicide at the expense of the state? Surely, if the Crown's lawyers believed Cross's confession they had an obligation to prevent him from taking that way out? But then, if they had tried to prevent Cross from hanging every future murderer would have claimed that he had done it as a form of suicide.

This is bizzare. Was the hanged man's "confession" the truth? He showed signs of conscience yet claimed that he had pursued a desperately violent stabbing attack on an almost total stranger. Was he insane? Probably not. All murder defendants are examined by a Home Office psychiatrist and any serious suggestion of insanity would have led the Home Secretary to intervene. Some people believe that Cross did not tell the truth, that something else took place in that parked car, something which made Cross profoundly ashamed and which, coupled with his wife's desertion, made him feel that he had no reason to live.

"Here master!
Here's a woman!"
(Moxley, Staffs, 1867)

All the world's civilisations have adopted religions of one form or another which set out moral codes they should live by to prevent strife and promote harmony. Given this, it is pitiful that religion has been used as an excuse for some of history's worst acts of violence. The long story of mankind is stained by the darkness of religious bigotry leading to mayhem, Catholic against Protestant, Jew against Muslim, Christian against pagan, Muslim against Hindu, all the way down to the present.

In mid 19th century Britain the main cause of religious violence was the Catholic/Protestant divide. The Catholic Emancipation Act of 1831 relieved Catholics of civil disabilities and so allowed them to stand for election and other public offices. It had not convinced people who harboured an irrational hatred of their fellow Christians. Then as now, there were demagogues willing to stir this hatred and create for themselves a power base. One such was a Protestant preacher from Northern Ireland called Murphy, head of an organisation known as the Knights of Saint George.

His home province was fertile ground, but Murphy decided to carry his vision to Scotland and England. His tour began in the industrial towns of west Scotland in 1867 and it was soon clear that his rabble rousing provoked violence wherever he spoke. Outbreaks became so predictable they were known as "Murphy riots".

His tour carried on southwards through Scotland, crossed into England and inflamed the northern manufacturing towns before making for the Midlands. By then Catholics in towns that this hysterical bigot was about to visit knew what to expect. Walsall Library has a series of posters published by the town's Catholic congregations when he was due to speak there. They warn in clear terms that where Murphy spoke Catholics might have to meet their Maker rather sooner than expected. What took place there is still remembered as the "Birchills Riots".

Murphy spoke in Wednesbury with an unusual result, the roof fell in. He might have seen that as a mark of divine disapproval, but he carried on and provoked the usual riot, followed by months of ill feeling.

The cash which financed this vicious circus came from sales of a propaganda book called *Secrets of the Confessional Unmasked*, a near pornographic account of what Roman Catholic priests were alleged to do to female parishioners in the confessional. There was nothing new about this kind of nonsense. Thirty or so years before there had been *The Awful Disclosures of Maria Monk*, which was supposed to tell the true story of the mistreatment of Miss Monk in a Canadian convent.

While the authorities deplored the violence that followed Murphy, they took no effective measures to prevent it until he went to Wolverhampton. The Justices of the Peace for that town were as unwilling as magistrates anywhere else to ban a religious speaker, but someone thought of a solution. They held a court hearing on the question of *Secrets of the Confessional*, decided that it was obscene and banned its sale in the town. Deprived of his main source of funding, Mr Murphy went home and was never heard of again, nor was his dirty book. The Maria Monk tale has done better. I bought my own paperback copy a few years ago in a respectable market town newsagent's shop where it shared the counter with detective novels, kids' comics and womens' magazines.

Murphy certainly left bitterness behind, but he may have left something more. On a Saturday morning late in November 1867 three boys, Tom Price, John Church and Samuel Church, were crossing a field by Broadwater's Colliery in Quarry Bank close to the Wednesbury turnpike (now Holyhead Road). There they came across a mound of clothing which they examined cautiously to find a bloodstained corpse. Rushing away to raise the alarm they met an elderly man, Moses Baggott Senior. "Here Master!" they called to him, "Here's a woman!" He went to look and recognised the corpse. She was his daughter in law, Esther Baggott, and he had been looking for her.

Esther's body was taken to the George Inn at Cock Heath, where it was examined by the Bilston surgeon, W.H. Hancox. Apart from coagulated blood on the face he found evidence that she had been strangled by a hand over her mouth and nostrils and abrasions about her jaw.

On the Monday following the discovery, the Coroner's Inquest sat at the George. Esther Baggott was 35 years old and for 15 years had been married to Moses Baggott Junior, a furnaceman at Monway Works in Wednesbury. Esther Davies, as she had been, had lived with her parents at Heathfield Bridge, Moxley, close to the Baggott family, but on her marriage she moved into their home.

The relationship was not a happy one, with both husband and wife suspecting each other of infidelity. Moses Junior had a boyhood sweetheart, Elizabeth Turner of King's Hill, Wednesbury, who had left him and emigrated to America. After his marriage Elizabeth returned and the old flame burned anew. His marriage didn't seem to make any difference. Esther was not very happy about this and six months before her death had been before the Justices to be bound over to keep the peace after a fight with "the American woman".

Esther's in laws were not much help. They seemed to prefer their son's old sweetheart to her and encouraged his adulterous relationship. Esther had gone back to her mother's home but returned to the Baggott household a few weeks before her death.

Whether Moses or Esther was the first to break the marriage vow we don't know, but it seems that she was involved with a boat builder called Edward Cauldwell who lived close to Baggott's Bridge.

Mary Davies, Esther's mother, and two of her friends, Martha Longmore and Mary Buckley, gave evidence at the Inquest. They told of Esther's unhappy marriage life, how she feared her father in law and called him a "nasty man" and how her husband was violent to her, breaking her nose at Wednesbury Wakes in September.

Esther's mother also said that Edward Cauldwell had called at her home seeking Esther about a month before. Told that she had returned to her husband, he slammed a knife into the table and declared that he would kill Esther if he didn't see her soon. He had also called on the day of the murder, saying that he wanted to see Esther, "in secret".

Caudwell said that on the crucial Friday evening he had left work with a friend, Edward Jones, and they had gone to a beerhouse kept by Mr Bowers, son in law of Moses Senior. Esther had called in about 7.00 pm with a watch she was bringing back from Bilston for the old man. She took a jug of beer for her husband's supper and left. Caudwell had returned to his boat for a wash but was back at the pub about 8.00 and stayed for several hours, as a number of witnesses confirmed.

Leaving Bowers's beerhouse, Esther had walked a mile or so to Monway Works with Moses's supper. She got there about 8.00 and was met at the gate by John Farnell, Moses's apprentice. She mentioned to him that a couple of Moses's friends had been fishing but didn't catch any bait, only a pair of small pike. This was because Moses was coming off shift at 2 o'clock in the morning and intended fishing the next day.

Going home, Esther had looked into James Whitehouse's beerhouse in Portway Road and had a half of ale with Martha Longmore. They left together and Martha, who lived nearby, had asked Esther in for supper. She had refused, saying that Moses Senior would be angry with her if she was late and that she had to get her husband's clothes ready for his fishing trip. Martha had escorted her as far as the Nelson Inn on Portway Road.

Just before 9 o'clock as she was making her way towards Moxley, Esther met another friend. She appeared anxious to get home. Mary Buckley told the Inquest how she and Esther had walked the road a few nights earlier and seen some roughs hanging about in the shadows, which seemed to disturb Esther greatly.

The time of Esther's death may have been fixed by William Evans, a sinker from Cock Heath. He and a friend had been waiting to go down the pit in Broadwater's Field at about 9 o'clock when they heard screams. Evans had ignored them, saying to his friend, "The bank wenches are prowling around, seemingly". He may well have heard Esther's last cries.

That she was attacked by the road was established from a pool of blood. She had then been dragged into the field. She was not robbed, for a watch and chain hung about her neck, and she was not sexually assaulted. What then was the motive for the murder of Esther Baggott?

****

The Coroner's Jury must have had serious problems. At first glance there were three good suspects. Moses Junior might have killed her out of anger or to clear the way to marry his Elizabeth, but he was at Monway Works. Edward Caudwell might have killed out of anger or frustration at her return to her husband, but he was at Bowers's beerhouse with lots of witnesses. "Nasty" old Moses Senior might have killed her, but why?

These were days when Coroners' Juries did not hesitate to name individuals in their verdicts. This counted under the law of the time as an indictment, that is, that the accused had a case to answer, so they would stand trial. In Esther Baggott's case they baulked at that responsibility and produced a verdict of "Murder by a person or persons unknown", and no one was ever arrested.

Shortly after her death her husband and his two brothers moved to Sheffield where, early in 1869, he married his boyhood love, Elizabeth Turner. She did not live long because the 1881 Census shows a Moses Baggott living with a wife called Harriet, presumably his third.

So, who killed Esther Baggott? Moses Junior, Cauldwell, or nasty old Moses Senior for the motives mentioned above? Or was it something else entirely? Moses Junior later said that Esther was killed to silence her. Why? Because she knew something important about the death of an elderly woman during the "Murphy riots" in Wednesbury. Was that why he moved to Sheffield, because he also knew? Or was he involved in the riot death?

The problems surrounding the murder of Esther Baggott will probably stay unsolved, but it seems possible that the unpleasant Mr Murphy left behind in Wednesbury more than religious illwill.

"It was something
I really hated."
(Baslow, Chesterfield
and W.Germany 1960-61)

The dumpy little imported cars that pre-dated the Mini became popular in the late 1950s with people who couldn't afford a saloon and didn't want to ride a motor bike. Like the Mini, they had relatively large cabins and small engine compartments, but they were less well designed. The huge area of window made them look dumpy and comical, like bubbles in fact. Until outclassed by the British Mini these little Heinkels and Messerschmitts were much loved and much ridiculed. I remember a joke from the heatwave summer of 1959, "A bubble car drew up and two fried eggs got out."

The press love to seize on some topical aspect of a crime to make a headline, so the murder of William Elliott became "The Bubble Car Murder".

Sixty year old William Elliott's body was found on 12th June 1960 in Clod Hill Lane, a lonely way that crosses the moors near Baslow, Derbyshire. He had died of serious head injuries. His bubble car was missing but was found crashed in Park Road, Chesterfield with Elliott's shoes inside.

Three days after the discovery of Elliott's body a 51 one year old bus cleaner approached the police. He had been attacked a week before Elliott's death in Boythorpe Road, which is in the area where the bubble car was found. William Atkinson looked very much like William Elliott and the two men sometimes drank in the Spread Eagle pub. Detective Superintendent Leonard Stretton, in charge of the inquiry, began to wonder if Atkinson had been attacked by mistake.

After three more days Mrs Gladys Vickers told the police that she had seen William Elliott the night before his corpse was found. She knew Elliott and had seen him being chased along an alley outside the Royal Oak public house. The pursuer was dark haired and swarthy with thin features and had caught up with him. Then she heard someone say "Oh", and groan.

The inquest on William Elliott showed that he had been kicked to death and returned a verdict of, "murder by a person or persons unknown". Superintendent Stretton's team took thousands of witness statements but made no arrest.

****

In the spring of the following year, on 29th March 1961, another body was found in Clod Hill Lane.

Once again the victim was a middle aged man, a 48 year old Chesterfield chemist called George Gerald Stobbs. His car was missing but was found abandoned in exactly the same place as Elliott's car.

The press began to refer to the second killing as a copycat murder, but the police thought it was more probably a second killing by the same killer. Now also, they could see how the murderer's victims were selected. Both Elliott and Stobbs had friends in common and drank in the Three Horseshoes pub. Both were homosexuals.

The investigation dragged on. Plainclothes police were sent to mingle with drinkers in the Three Horseshoes. More witness statements were taken. There were rumours of a third murder. Sixty-three year old Arthur Jenkinson was been questioned by Stretton's team and found dead shortly afterwards with his head in a gas oven. The inquest verdict was suicide, but a rumour persisted that Jenkinson had been overcome and had his head forced into the oven.

Meanwhile, far away in West Germany on November 1960, a young German soldier, Guenther Helmbrecht, was murdered in a forest near Verden.

There was large British Army camp nearby and as a matter of routine the German police asked for a list of soldiers who were off the camp on the day of the murder. One of the officers who handled the list was a Derbyshire man whose family sent him the local papers, so he knew about the unsolved murders at Chesterfield. He saw on the list of soldiers out of camp when Guenther Helmbrecht was killed, the name of a soldier who also came from Derbyshire.

This connection led eventually to the arrest of 26 year old Michael Copeland. In a confession, later retracted, he said that homosexuality "was something I really hated", marking himself as one of those wretched people who can only cope with the guilt of their own sexuality by beating or killing their sexual partners.

He was tried and convicted for the murders of Elliott, Stobbs and Helmbrecht and normally would have hanged for the Derbyshire killings. Luckily for him, West Germany had no death penalty and would only extradite a wanted killer to Britain against a guarantee that they would not suffer a greater penalty than in Germany. As a result, Copeland's sentence was commuted to life imprisonment.

"You and I shall have a dance together."
(Rugby, Warwickshire 1781)

Duelling, or settling a dispute with swords or pistols, has long been illegal in Britain, but it still went on well into the 19th century. Many prominent people allowed themselves to get involved in this peculiar and often fatal game. These two stories are linked by a duel in a London hotel and feature lords and ladies, rascally army officers, two heiresses, a fighting parson and a murder trial in Warwick.

You will have seen enough duels on TV or films to have a good idea of the routine. Cause for offence having been given (or, at least, offence being taken) the insulted would issue a challenge. The insultor could apologize and afterwards be deemed a coward, or take up the challenge.

The parties and their seconds would then gather at some concealed place, often at dawn, and the ritual would follow long established rules. If everybody was lucky there would be a minor injury, honour would be satisfied, and the whole party could go off to a drunken breakfast before the law galloped out of the trees. If someone was killed or seriously injured, then someone else would be galloping for the Channel ferry.

****

In the London of 1777 it was not surprising to find a young army officer and a journalist fighting a duel. What was surprising was that they fought with pistols in a room of Osborne's Hotel near the Strand.

At this time half-pay officers of the Army and Navy, that is, those still in service but without a posting to ship or regiment, were much addicted to duelling. They seem to have treated it as a way of keeping up their fighting skills. So the involvement of Captain Andrew Stoney was no surprise, but the other figure in the drama was the Reverend Henry Bate.

Captain Stoney was the son of a Tipperary squire who lived at Coldpighill in County Durham. He had recently been paying court to the widowed Lady Strathmore whose first marriage had lasted only a year and left her young and enormously rich. Even before her husband's death she had been receiving visits from the Honorable George Grey and her widowhood seems to have increased Grey's enthusiasm.

You would not expect to find a clergyman fighting duels, but the Reverend Henry Bate was no ordinary cleric. The son of a parson, he was ordained but took to journalism, and for some years he was connected with the *Morning Post* before founding his own newspaper.

Items in the *Morning Post* had suggested that George Grey's relationship with Lady Strathmore was not as honorable as his title. Captain Stoney was outraged at this slur on the lady's honour and challenged Parson Bate.

A TEW

The *Annual Review* reported events at Osborne's Hotel; how Bate and Stoney had fired pistols at each other without any injury but had then drawn swords to continue. Stoney was wounded in the chest and arm and Bate in the thigh. Bate protested that his sword had become bent when he struck Stoney's breastbone and Stoney allowed him to straighten it. As he was doing so the locked door was forced by outsiders anxious to end the battle and hotel guests disturbed by pistol shots and swordplay. Honour was apparently satisfied.

So far so suitably melodramatic. The immediate outcome was that Bate agreed not to issue further slurs on Lady Strathmore and she wrote to Captain Stoney expressing undying love. Within four days they were married, though she dined with Honorable George on her wedding eve.

It might all come from a romantic novel but for one thing. The libels, the challenge and the duel were a fake set up between Bate and Stoney to win the lady's heart and drive George Grey out of the bidding. Years later Stoney's valet swore an affidavit recording that when the door was forced a doctor was bleeding Stoney's arm and there was no blood "but what came from the lancet". There were holes in the Captain's waistcoat but not his shirt, and Parson Bate's breeches were torn on the thigh, though this appeared to have been done "with a hot poker". Neither of the seconds had been in the room during the "duel", but when Captain Donellan, Bate's second, arrived he was put out about the point of his sword being bent.

If the duel was a ruse to trap Lady Strathmore, it worked, but not entirely to Captain Stoney's satisfaction. In those days the fortune of a married woman became the property of her husband on marriage, but the Honorable George thwarted Stoney by suggesting to Lady Strathmore a way of protecting her wealth. She may have rushed into marriage with her gallant Captain, but she paused on the way to execute a trust deed giving the trustees complete power over her fortune and reserving it for her own use. Stoney, who changed his name to Bowes to satisfy Lady Strathmore's family, discovered this only after the wedding.

Stoney tried persuasions, like keeping his wife indoors and blacking her eyes, until on 1st May she revoked the trust. This did not restore matrimonial harmony, so Bowes continued to mistreat her until, in 1785, she started divorce proceedings on the grounds of cruelty and adultery.

English law did not allow divorce until the 1930s but there was a strange and expensive procedure used by the wealthy. It was (and is) possible for Parliament to pass a personal and private act to end the marriage of a particular couple, or to do anything else for that matter, if you can persuade the law makers that it is a good thing. Some years ago such an Act was passed to permit the marriage of an elderly man and the equally elderly but unrelated daughter of his deceased wife. Most Acts apply to everyone, everywhere, but private ones affect only particular people or companies. By 1785 there were private acts creating toll road companies and giving them powers to build roads and charge people for using them. All the canal and railway companies were created in this way, not least because they needed compulsory purchase powers to acquire land.

Private bills have always started in the House of Lords where the main part of the procedure is a committee hearing at which barristers for the promoters and objectors put their cases, quite like a court hearing.

Bowes hired a team of thugs and set a watch on his wife, eventually arranging her kidnap in London. Lady Strathmore was dragged as a prisoner all the way to Bowes's Durham property of Streatlam Castle where she was kept prisoner and shuttled back and forth between Penrith and Newcastle. At last she was rescued and began a criminal prosecution against her husband. This put him and some of his henchmen in jail and was followed by a case disputing the validity of her revocation of the trust deed. Bowes died in prison in 1810 and his wife followed him in 1820.

Parson Bate was imprisoned in 1781 for libeling the Duke of Richmond. Some years later he took on the name of Dudley, though his friends still called him Parson Bate. In 1797 he purchased a church living, that is, a post as a vicar with an income from church lands. The bishop smelled corruption and refused to ratify the appointment, but there were other bishops. He acquired several such livings in Ireland and pursued a clerical career so successfully that in 1813 he was made a baronet. Four years later he was made a prebendary of Ely Cathedral, that is, a member of the ecclesiastical staff, with a living. Parson Bate died in 1824, full of years and wealth and seemingly at peace with church and state.

✷✷✷✷✷✷✷

There is another story linked to the Osborne Hotel duel. The young army officer who was second to Parson Bate and was put out about the sword being bent was Captain Donellan, late of the 39th Regiment of Foot and hence on half pay. He had served in the East Indies with the army of the East India Company where he earned dishonour after the capture of Masulipatam by his dealings with Indian merchants. Returning to England he succeeded in convincing the Army that he remained an officer and a gentleman and was allowed to retain his commission on half pay. He was in this reduced state at Osborne's Hotel.

Engraving of Captain John Donellan from the *European Magazine* 1st May 1781.

When the duelling and marrying were over the young Captain took himself to Bath where, apart from the ogling, flirting and seductions you can read about in Jane Austen's books, there were card games and money to be won.

We do not know about Donellan's luck at cards, but his luck in love was in when he was able to be of service to the Dowager Lady Boughton and her daughter Theodosia.

Bath still is a fairly small town, so that the annual invasion of mothers with marriageable daughters and young men looking for a chance caused accommodation problems. Lady Boughton and daughter had not reserved a room and found that they might have to pass their first night in Bath sleeping on chairs in the coffee lounge. The suave and gallant Captain Donellan offered them his own room and slept on a chair.

It was a courteous act and even a watchful mother felt obliged to respond. Donellan was invited to breakfast with the Boughtons and from there acquaintance ripened. Soon the Captain was arranging excursions for the ladies and accompanying them everywhere. Even so, he was only a half-pay Captain and Theodosia was an heiress. Marriage with the consent of their chaperone, the Dowager Lady Boughton, was impossible, so they eloped.

Lady Boughton returned home to Lawford Hall, near Rugby, in solitary fury and forbade her daughter and her husband the house. Her son, the Baronet Sir Theodosius Boughton, was less hostile. He made several visits to his sister and her Captain at Bath, where Donellan advised Sir Theo and tried to keep him out of various scrapes.

The young baronet was an unpleasant youth who had been expelled from Eton for his vices. This was long before the 19th century reformation of the English public schools made them the educational powerhouse of the late Victorian Empire. At this time they were conveniences for the aristocracy, where they might send their unruly sons to do their unpleasant and disorganised growing up away from the family. At Eton boys from 9 to 19 mingled in a society that was largely unsupervised and unregulated, where bullying, drunkenness, womanising and sodomy were commonplace. It must have taken exceptional talent to be expelled.

Whether because of the good offices of her brother, Theodosia was at last forgiven and she and her Captain were accepted as residents at Lawford Hall. Donellan's career seemed to have reached a safe haven, though the Dowager made it a term of the reconciliation that Donellan should agree never to set his hands upon his wife's fortune, a term which he accepted.

Lawford Hall near Rugby stood by a mill at Little Lawford by the River Avon. The Hall was demolished in the 1790s and all that remains is a fishpond and the stables. The mill building is now a farm.

The new arrangements at Lawford Hall began in June 1778. The Baronet who was newly expelled from Eton confessed to Donellan that he had a venereal infection and had consulted a quack, as a result of which he was taking mercury.

Captain Donellan was worried about his Sir Theo's health and urged Lady Broughton to employ reputable medical men. Ever a skinflint, she refused but gave her son a medical textbook called *The Family Physician*, which was about as useful as flinging a lighted match into straw.

Young Theo set about being his own doctor with enthusiasm, poring over the book and dreaming up wonderful remedies to try on himself. None of them worked. He lost weight, he slobbered and shook. When Doctor Powell of Rugby finally saw him he found a large, blackening swelling in the boy's groin and opined that the Baronet had the "venereal virus in his blood". Once a headstrong bully, Theo now wept cravenly, the hand of death on his shoulder, and swore to repent and lead a better life if he got well.

He did not get well but he improved slightly, so that on 29th August 1778 he decided to go fishing. Captain Donellan opposed the project fearing that Theo would catch a chill, but the boy would not be stopped.

While Theo angled a servant was sent to collect another bottle of medicine from Rugby. It was fetched and left in Sir Theodosius's room, labelled "For the purging of Mr Boughton". It was a standard mixture of the day, a compound of rhubarb, jalap, nutmeg, spirits of lavender and syrup, not much good perhaps, but not much harm.

On the next morning, 30thAugust, Captain Donellan had agreed to escort Lady Boughton to Rugby to interview a prospective servant. He waited on horseback at the front of the Hall until he received a message that the Dowager was not yet ready. He then trotted off to King's Newham to take the medicinal water of a chalybeate spring.

When he returned the Hall was in disorder. The Dowager called to him from the window of Theo's bedroom and the Captain ran up to find his brother in law dead in bed. Donellan took command at once. When Lady Boughton explained that she had given her son a dose of the bottled remedy, the Captain smelt it, tasted it on his finger and poured it out into a basin of water, saying that it smelt and tasted bitter. He ordered the clearing and cleaning of the room and sent for surgeons to see the body.

On 4[th]September they had a whole battalion of surgeons. From Coventry came David Rattray and Bradford Wilmer, from Warwick, David Geary Snow and from Rugby, Samuel Bucknill. They all agreed that the body was so putrefied that they could not determine the cause of death, but that the mixture given him on the morning of his demise could not have caused it. Lady Boughton refused to pay their fees and Donellan eventually had to foot the bill because he had sent for them.

On 6th September Sir Theodosius was buried and gossip began about his death, including reflections on the competence of the covey of surgeons. Theo had hardly settled into his grave when he was exhumed to be re-examined by Dr Bucknill, dressed in vinegar-soaked clothing. He found no inflammation of the stomach such as he would have expected from poisoning, but a great deal of blood in the chest. He took a sample of stomach fluid and fed it to his dog which suffered no harm, so almost certainly neutralising the idea of arsenic poisoning.

Theo was returned to his rest but the rumours went on, focussing on Donellan. On 14th September 1780 the gallant Captain was arrested, charged with murdering his brother in law by administering arsenic in laurel water and taken in chains to Warwick gaol. There he languished, protesting his innocence, until the trial began on 30th March 1781.

✱✱✱✱✱✱✱

Lady Boughton was the best prosecution witness. She told the Court that Donellan had ordered the clearing and cleaning of her son's room and had emptied all the medicine bottles. The maid, Sarah Blundell, had been present but had since died in childbirth. Lady Boughton even came close to dragging her daughter into suspicion, claiming to have heard the Captain and his wife discussing his concern when he realised that the medicine smelt and tasted bitter.

In the witness box Lady Boughton was asked to smell a bottle of the supposed purging mixture and a bottle of the same with laurel water added. She said that the second smelt like the potion she had given her son, of bitter almonds. It had caused a "prodigious rattling" of Theo's stomach, followed by gurgling, clenched teeth and foaming at the mouth. She had remonstrated with Donellan when he emptied the bottle but he claimed it was so that he could taste the mixture. Two doctors said that from Lady Boughton's description the cause of death was poisoning by laurel water, which contains cyanide.

Witnesses said that the Captain kept a still and made laurel water, which he admitted. He distilled rose water and lavender water for the servants to sponge the bedding to keep fleas at bay, and he distilled laurel water as an aromatic footbath.

Donellan pointed out Theo's practice of doping himself with self invented remedies and his use of arsenic. He had once asked Donellan to bring him a pound of powdered arsenic from Coventry. The Captain was worried by the amount and Theo's carelessness and brought only a 4 ounce slab. Theo flew into a rage and sent a servant to Rugby to have the arsenic pounded into powder. The poison was ostensibly to kill rats though it was also used as a sexual stimulant. Theo had joked with Lady Boughton about his carelessness, saying that he must be careful not to mix arsenic with his medicines. Lady Boughton had admitted to Donellan that she had poisoned her husband's dogs with arsenic.

As to motive, Captain Donellan had no reason at all to kill Theodosius. He had already and willingly agreed not to touch the Broughton fortune, but Theodosius had the gift of two clerical livings. He had suggested that when the elderly incumbents retired he should assign them to Donellan to provide him with a good income. By his death Donellan had lost this benefit.

The Captain had often rescued young Theo from lunatic scrapes, like the occasion when he tried to climb the tower of Newbold on Avon church, and at the time of the death he had been well away from Lawford Hall.

None of this helped him at all, nor lack of any evidence that Theo had died of poisoning. Captain Donellan was found guilty and sentenced to death.

To the end he remained gallant. A contemporary account tells how he laid out the cap which he would wear to be hanged and said to it, "You and I shall have a dance together on Monday".

A charming engraving from one of the popular broadsheets of the day.

The Captain was hanged in the Saltisford, Warwick at dawn on 2nd April 1781. The hangman apologised for the early appointment, which was caused by his having two further executions that day in Birmingham.

In his last letter to his wife Donellan urged her to leave Lawford Hall and implied that he suspected Lady Boughton of the murder. Theodosia took his advice and left Lawford to marry Sir Egerton Leigh and raise a second family. Her will left everything to her children by Donellan, but they died before her. Her daughter died of natural causes but her son hanged himself at his public school when a fellow pupil taunted him with being the son of a murderer.

The case has been much written about. The great William Roughead believed Donellan was guilty, so did Jack Smith-Hughes. More modern writers exonerate him for the reasons I have suggested. Some believe that he was convicted because of social prejudice against a half pay officer of no breeding who had carried off an heiress, a victim of snobbery. If he didn't do it, who or what killed Sir Theodosius Boughton?

"I wonder how much insurance I shall get."
(Kingstanding, Birmingham 1951)

From our stressed, polluted, drugged, crime haunted present some people look back at the years after World War II as a golden age. Television series set in those years suggest that everybody was nice to everybody, crime was unknown outside Dock Green, every mother could cook and bake, all wives were faithful, drugs did not exist and the (steam) railways ran on time.

Gosh Grandad, was it really like that? Of course not. The early 1950s may have been more pleasant in many ways, but pollution was worse than it is now, and we had poverty, stress, sexual infidelity, drugs, chokingly dirty old trains that ran late - and crime.

When the wisdom, decency or efficacy of hanging murderers began to be debated in the 1950s there were plenty of people who believed that hanging was the only way to prevent everyone being murdered in their beds. They overlooked the fact that murder is the least repeated offence. If you wanted to use hanging to prevent repeated crimes it would be more effective to hang people who steal cars.

When hanging was abolished the predicted rise in the murder rate did not happen, it went on falling. It has risen slightly in recent years but we still have by far the lowest murder rate of any developed nation.

Nowadays there is much less public demand for hanging but the murder of a child usually brings out those in favour. What would the modern public or our tabloid press make of four murders of little girls within a few weeks?

****

On 8th July 1951, 7 year old Christine Butcher went missing in Windsor. Her body was found the next day in a meadow by the Thames. She had been sexually assaulted and suffocated.

A week later, on 15th July, 6 year old Brenda Goddard of Bath was reported missing but found three hours later in a copse behind her home.

On 9th August Cicely Batstone went missing from her home in Bath. Twenty four hours later she was found strangled in a field near the Wells road.

Between the deaths of Brenda Goddard and Cicely Batstone there had been another killing, this time in Birmingham. Four children had been murdered in thirty one days of one summer, almost one a week.

On 23rd July, eight days after Brenda Goddard's death, her foster mother, Mrs Pullen, received a letter which had been posted at Birmingham:

> "I want to say how sorry I am for what I did to your daughter. I don't know what made me do it, but it is too late now. But I can say within the next two weeks they will find my body somewhere."

The letter was signed, "H.R.G" and a postscript warned, "There may be another murder within that two weeks". The police could not make any sensible connection between this letter and the murder of Brenda Goddard.

On 1st August, eight days after receipt of the letter, 11 year old Sheila Attwood went missing from Caversham Road, Kingstanding. The alarm was raised rapidly because Mrs Attwood made a practise of getting her nine children to bed by 6.30 every evening.

Sheila, it appeared, had been in the local park at 2 o'clock that afternoon, paddling with a friend. At four they had left the park to go home but Sheila changed her mind and said that she was going back there.

Police and neighbours searched the area but were hampered by darkness and Sheila was not found. At about noon the next day one of Sheila's schoolfriends, Doreen Ford, went into the garden with her mother and they saw Sheila's legs protruding from under the privet hedge at the bottom of the garden Her body had been dumped on a Birmingham Corporation yard behind the house. On the same evening the police announced that a man had been detained in connection with Sheila's murder.

Horace Carter, a 32 year old labourer from Caversham Road, Kingstanding, appeared in Birmingham Magistrates' Court on 3rd August before the redoubtable stipendiary magistrate, Mr JF Milward. The prosecution was represented by the equally redoubtable Mervyn P Pugh, agent in Birmingham for the Director of Public Prosecutions.

Offered legal aid by the Stipendiary, Carter said, "No, sir, I don't think it's worth it'" The case was adjourned until 6th September. The Coroner's Inquest began on the same day but was adjourned to 28th September.

When Carter reappeared before Stipendiary Milward, Mervyn Pugh asserted, "The motive for the crime was lust, followed by fear that the girl might tell someone what he had done to her and, accordingly, he murdered her. He lived next door."

On 1st August Carter's brother in law had gone out of the house for a while. According to Carter's confession, he had came back to the empty house and found Sheila Attwood standing near the back door holding onto his bike. He invited her into the front room and gave her sweets, then asked her to go up to his bedroom. In the bedroom he sexually assaulted the girl, then strangled her. He left her body in the bedroom until his brother in law had gone to bed, then took it down to the Corporation yard.

He concluded, "I am extremely sorry for what I did, and so ought to get topped. There isn't any more to put down except I am glad it is all over".

In police custody Carter had remarked, "I don't know why I did it. Wish I could put the clock back forty eight hours. It's no good talking now, it's too late". He also said, "I wonder how much insurance I shall get if I get my neck stretched. I am in an endowment."

Chief Inspector Harris referred in his evidence to a book called *Famous Detective Stories* found in Carter's room. The Stipendiary questioned whether it should be included as an exhibit.

Mr Wynschenk for the defence said, "I should be sorry to feel that possession of detective stories is indicative of guilt. I don't think it is relevant, but I don't think it is a matter I can object to".

Mr Pugh said that he thought "it might be beneficial to the defence later on", an astonishing remark from someone who never willingly gave the defence an advantage.

The same queries were raised later over another book, *Mistress of Murder*, found at Carter's home. Carter was committed for trial at Birmingham Assizes, where he was subsequently found insane.

****

The two Bath killings led eventually to the arrest of a man called John Straffen who was found unfit to plead and committed to Broadmoor. He later escaped and struck again.

The late 20th and early 21st centuries have been called The Age of Anxiety, not least because of the feeling that crime has reached unparalleled heights, and especially crimes against children. It will not reassure worried parents to hear about events in 1951, but objectively it seems that things are no worse now.

"After many strange excuses.."
(Leek, Staffs, 1678)

Blake Mere, also known as the Mermaid's Pool, lies about 7 miles from Leek near the Buxton Road. Nineteenth century legend told of a mermaid who lived in the pool and lured men to their deaths. She is also alleged to have told someone that if the pool was ever emptied she would "drown all Leek and Leek-Frith".

The scaly seductress is remembered in the name of the Mermaid Inn, previously Blackmere House, which may once have been a drovers' inn.

"Black Mere" is not only the old name of the pub, but also of the pool, "'the Black Mere of Morridge", and quite apart from any fishy residents, it had an unwholesome reputation. In 1686 Dr Robert Plott wrote his *Natural History of Staffordshire*, describing the Moorlands as a place of noisome "boggs", peat cuttings full of stagnant water and "contagious vapors". Even so, he was scornful of the Black Mere's reputation:

The "Black Pool of Morridge" is a small blue pool in the heather and rough grass on the edge of the moorland above Leek. The views are wide and magnificent. Below is The Mermaid Inn, hunched against the bitter wind.

"Yet are not these neither so bad as some have fancyed the water is of the black-Meer of Morridge, which I take to be nothing more than such as those in the peat-pits; though it be confidently reported that no Cattle will drink of it, no bird light on it, or fly over it; all of which are as false as that it is bottomlesse; it being found upon measure scarce four yards in the deepest place, my Horse also drinking when I was there as freely as I ever saw Him at any other place, and the fowle so far from declining to fly over it, that I spake with several that had seen Geese upon it; so that I take this to be as good as the rest, notwithstanding the vulgar disrepute it lyes under".

Despite the good Doctor's scientific opinions about the nature and depth of the water and the behaviour of the wildlife, I am surprised that nobody told so enthusiastic a gossip as Plott that a few years before he investigated the Mere someone had dropped a body into it.

✷✷✷✷✷✷✷

In 1677 Andrew Sympson, a former cobbler, was a young ostler at the Red Lion Inn, Leek. One September day a Staffordshire farmer came to Leek market and left his horse in Andrew's care. The farmer's corn sold for £3, a goodly sum in those days, so that when the market closed he returned to the Red Lion and drank some of his profits until darkness fell. About 10 o'clock he tipped the young ostler 2 pence [just under 1p] and set off on the 4 mile ride to his home.

What made Andrew Sympson greedy we don't know, but he certainly decided that the farmer's purse held more than it did and that he was going to have it. Taking a horse from the Red Lion's stable, he rode by a shortcut to confront the farmer in the dark on a lonely stretch of moorland.

Taking the countryman's purse, Sympson tied the man hand and foot with a horse halter, drove off his horse and left his victim to pass a cold and penniless night on the ground.

Early next day travellers found the farmer and brought him back to Leek, but he failed to recognise the Red Lion's ostler as his attacker and no suspicion whatever attached to the youth.

Secure in the success of his first highway robbery, though it had not netted as much as he had hoped, Andrew bided his time until about March of the following year. Then a young man passed through Leek on his way to Nantwich, staying overnight at the Red Lion. This gave the thieving ostler the opportunity to note that the guest was well provided with money, so he generously offered to show the young man the road to Congleton for a mile or two.

They set out early the next morning and had not gone more than a few miles when Sympson attacked his companion and robbed him of money, gold and silver rings and a silver box. Then he beat the traveller to death.

Once more he returned to Leek, better satisfied this time with the fruits of his crime. He told people that he had separated from the traveller quite a short distance from Leek and, again, was not suspected of the crime.

He was careful enough to sell the silver box and the rings in Stafford, not Leek, saying that he had found them. He was not careful with the proceeds. Broadsheets were an early form of popular newspaper, and a contemporary one reported: "Andrew upon this Theft was full of money, which he spent freely, the only way to be poor again, and so be tempted to another sin".

Temptation did not wait long. In May a woman pedding lace, cloths and threads passed through Leek on her sales round. She had done well in previous towns and did well in Leek, so that when she set out for Bakewell at 3 o'clock one afternoon she had a good sum of money.

The murderous ostler knew that the lady's route would take her close to the lonely Black Mere at about nightfall and set out after her. On the banks of the dark water he attacked and strangled her, tied her body to a boulder and toppled it into the evil pool.

Andrew Sympson took her purse and her stock boxes and was home before dawn, hiding his loot in a haystack. Yet again, no suspicion attached to him. No body being found, nobody suspected that the pedlar had not gone on her intended way into Derbyshire.

Sympson's bloody career might have continued indefinitely. The Scottish cannibal, Sawney Beane, and his horrible clan, murdered and ate travellers on the moors of lowland Scotland for decades before they were discovered by accident.

Sympson was not so lucky. After the murder of the pedlar he was foolish enough to tell a serving maid at the inn that he would give her some lace. He seems to have realised his mistake, but she kept him to his word and nagged at him until he agreed to stump up. Still he did not have the sense to give her money instead, but went to his haystack stash and retrieved a piece of lace.

The girl was intrigued about the source of the lace and followed Sympson to see it taken from the haystack. She said nothing to him but that night she told a fellow servant girl. She in turn told her mistress, landlady of the Red Lion, who sent for Andrew and demanded an explanation. Sympson denied everything, so the landlady told her husband, who searched the haystack to find the lace and some of the money.

The broadsheet went on:

> "Andrew was secured and carried before a Justice, where after many strange excuses, he confesses the Fact, and for it, being committed to the Gaol, he was, this last Assizes there held, Condemn'd. And then he confessed to the other two facts, receiving the Just Reward of his horrible Murders and Robberies. This relation is known to be true by most of the inhabitants of Staffordshire, and by the Authors here inserted, Mr Tho.Hortley and Mr Samuel Stains".

Pheasant Hall is now the comfortable, rural home of Mr and Mrs Richardson. From the garden there are views of the Welsh mountains.

"We shall suffer wrongful"
(Audley, Staffs, 1844)

Murder in the Midlands (Quercus 2000) included a murder during the so called "poaching wars" which bedevilled rural England for much of the 19th century. Today we look at poaching as the eccentric hobby of a few rural individualists who cling to a dying craft. A hundred and fifty years ago it was in deadly earnest, very deadly.

Poaching was almost a necessity for the rural poor to supplement their meagre diet and earn a few shillings. It was also a way of expressing their contempt of their wealthy, land owning rulers. To their masters it was a sin against property, the worst kind, one that merited transportation and sometimes death.

Landowners employed monstrous mantraps which crippled their victims as well as gamekepers and assistants. All over the British countryside keepers and poachers confronted each other time and again in dark coverts and spinneys. Cudgels were raised and men were savagely beaten or maimed or killed by a shotgun. The dreadful penalty for being caught poaching only made it more likely that a poacher confronted by a gamekeeper would kill to save himself.

A gamekeeper who killed a poacher could always justify it. A poacher who killed a gamekeeper had raised the stakes from transportation to the gallows, but so great was the hostility between the two groups that many a keeper died or was injured by poachers. Hostility erupted even when keepers were not at work. They might be attacked and beaten senseless on their way home from the inn, their property would be stolen or damaged and sometimes they would be killed.

****

William Cooper was the son of a gamekeeper and helped his father, Thomas, in his work. Thomas kept the woods of Sir Thomas Boughey, and he and William lived in Pheasant Hall, a cottage by a small wood near Halmer End, Audley, just north-west of Newcastle under Lyme.

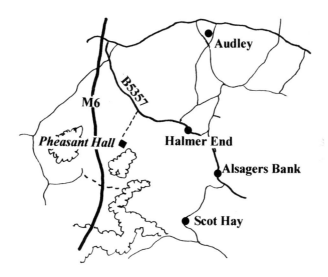

On a Sunday in August 1844 William Cooper went to a service at Audley's Methodist Chapel then took a drink with a friend at the King's Head. It was after dark at about 11 o'clock when he arrived at his own front door. As he lifted the latch a figure stepped from the shadows.

Cooper asked who it was but the only answer was the blast of a gun fired into his face. He cried out and collapsed on the doorstep. His father heard the shot and the cry and raced down to see what had happened only to find his son dying at his feet.

At daylight the Stoke on Trent police arrived. They searched the area and in the mud around the cottage found two sets of footprints. Major McKnight, in charge of the case, followed them across the fields until they petered out about a mile away in Scot Hay. The search also turned up a piece of torn blue paper which had evidently been used as a wad for the killer's shotgun.

McKnight had a suspect in mind, a poaching miner called Paul Downing. The cause of the Major's suspicion was the fact that Downing had been out of prison only two days after a two month sentence for trespassing, a conviction based on the evidence of Cooper and his father. It was widely known that Downing had sworn to avenge himself on the Coopers.

At noon on Monday the police called at Downing's home. He was drunk but they eventually managed to remove his boots. The soles were studded with distinctive large nails which matched the larger footprints leading away from the killing. Downing was arrested but swore he had passed the night at the home of his cousin, Charles Powis in Scot Hay.

The police called on Powis, but his support for Downing's alibi was so weak that they became suspicious of him. Looking at his bootsoles the police found a match for the smaller set of footprints at the murder scene. Better perhaps, a search of Powis's cottage unearthed a recently fired gun and a powder horn. The mouth of the powder horn was plugged with a wad of torn blue paper which precisely matched the wad found at the scene.

✻✻✻✻✻✻✻

At the Coroner's inquest Dr Davis, the Stoke on Trent police surgeon, told the court that William Cooper had many gunshot wounds in the face, upper body, left arm and hand. He did not believe that Cooper could have lived more than five minutes.

PC Basford said that he knew Downing. He had seen him at Alsager Bank in February where Downing was charged with poaching. He had escorted the miner to Burslem and handed him over to Superintendent Rowley. Rowley had said, "Paul, what are you doing here? You've been up to your old games again. I would advise you to give up this poaching for no good will come of it". Downing replied, "Mr Rowley, sir, I have been falsely accused".

Basford had also escorted Downing to Stafford when the collier was committed for trespass in pursuit of game, and on the way the prisoner had repeated the claim that he was falsely accused. He had sworn to take revenge on Cooper and his father. Downing had become violent so that Basford had difficulty restraining him, and he continued to curse the Coopers all the way to Stafford.

The Coroner's Jury named Downing and Powis as the wilful murderers of William Cooper and committed them for trial at Stafford. The Assize Jury heard the same evidence and convicted them both, though they could not determine which of them had actually fired the fatal shot.

Paul Downing declared, "If we suffer we shall suffer wrongful. We couldn't help what people said against us, or the jury bringing us in guilty, but we are as innocent as a child unborn". There was a local belief that Downing and Powis knew the killer's identity but would not buy their lives at that price.

They were hanged on 4th January 1845 when Downing made another declaration. "Within twelve months" he said, "you will know who the real culprits are and they'll be no better off than we are". Powis added, "I want to say something. Don't put the rope so tight. I can't breathe. We are going to die for a thing we know nothing about, and I hope the Lord in Heaven will protect us. We are going to suffer for that which we are innocent of".

As the hoods were placed over their heads they prayed aloud and were still praying when the trap dropped. Downing died immediately but Powis struggled for minutes.

****

A month later, on 1st February the *Staffordshire Advertiser* announced:

> "Since last Saturday no little excitement has been created in the neighbourhood of Newcastle by a report that some man has made a confession that he was the murderer of William Cooper. Many versions of the report obtained circulation all of which however are entirely destitute of the truth. They originated we understand in the extravagant and idiotic declaration of some drunken man in a public house".

And were Downing and Powis innocent? Well, there were the footprints, though those were never cast or photographed, only compared by human eye. Many boots must have had similar soles. There was the blue paper wad that matched the plug in Powis's powder horn and a local gunsmith confirmed that he had supplied the wads to Powis and Downing on the day before the shooting. Finally, there was Downing's loudly declared intention to revenge himself on Cooper. As good a case as any Victorian policeman or juror might wish.

Who was the drunk who "confessed"? It may have been a friend of the hanged men, another Audley poacher called Samuel Green. Just after the execution of his two friends, Samuel Green might well have had things on his mind that spilled over in drink. Nine years later he lay dying and this time his conscience hit him a harder. He confessed that he had borrowed Charles Powis's gun and used it to kill William Cooper. He never said who accompanied him.

What can you say of the courage and loyalty of Downing and Powis, facing the gallows rather than splitting on a friend, and what can you say of the craven friend who let them do it to save his own worthless skin?

"A cold confession of evil"
(Narborough, Leics 1983-1988)

The night of Monday 21st November 1983 was bitterly cold with a full moon. Around the Leicestershire village of Narborough a hard frost was whitening every surface under the bright moonlight.

At the Carlton Hayes Social Club there was a ladies' darts tournament, and Katherine and Eddie Eastwood spent part of their evening there before moving on to more darts at the Dog and Gun. They had a pleasant evening and arrived home at about 1.30 am.

Eddie's stepdaughter, Susan, was waiting up to tell them that her 15 year old sister, Lynda, had not come home.

The police were called but were not very concerned about a teenager who had stayed out. Eddie Eastwood went out searching for his stepdaughter but found nothing.

Alongside the village of Narborough lies a complex of Edwardian buildings that was once the Leicestershire and Rutland Lunatic Asylum, renamed Carlton Hayes Hospital. At 7.20 on Tuesday morning a hospital porter taking a path by the hospital known as the Black Pad saw something lying in the hospital grounds. With an ambulance driver who was just arriving for work they peered through the fence, wondering if what they saw was a dummy.

The driver found the gate at the end of the path wide open and approached the crumpled figure. It was not a mannequin; it was the body of Lynda Mann. She had been sexually assaulted and strangled.

****

By 8.30 am Chief Superintendent Baker, head of Leicestershire CID, was at the scene, beginning the first ever murder hunt in quiet Narborough and one that was to become a landmark in criminal investigation.

The police soon learned that Lynda had expected to babysit on Monday evening but the arrangement had been cancelled. Instead she had called on a friend. Her friend remembered that Lynda had left about 7.30 pm, just before the Coronation Street theme on TV. She would have walked home along the path by the cemetery and the hospital, the Black Pad.

Enquiries showed that Lynda was not sexually active, had no particular boyfriend and was well liked. She was a level headed, amiable girl, who was interested in languages and wanted to travel. Nothing in her private life gave any clue to her death.

The police knew that they were looking for a young male, rapists are almost always between their teens and their mid thirties, and they thought they were looking for a local man. Who else would be about the Black Pad on a bitter winter's night?

The post mortem showed that Lynda had not been raped. The attacker had ejaculated prematurely, and it was the semen that gave the first real clue. The perpetrator was a Group A secretor, meaning that he was of blood group A and that his blood group could be identified from other bodily fluids. Further analysis revealed that he belonged to a sub group of A secretors identified as PGM 1+. Blood group A includes about ten per cent of English males, but not all are secretors and not all are PGM 1+. The test could not positively identify the culprit but it could eliminate suspects.

The first suspect arrested was Eddie Eastwood, on the basis that most English murder victims are killed by someone in their immediate circle. He had a firm alibi and, anyway, he was not a PGM 1+.

A team of thirty police officers worked on the case operating out of a building loaned by Carlton Hayes Hospital, a hospital that treated, among many others, sex offenders. Nearby stood a building known as The Woodland which was a day centre for patients with minor mental problems. Local teenagers used it as a drop in centre and Lynda had been there more than once with others. It was close to her home and close to the Black Pad.

There were reports to follow up. A driver reported a youth and a girl at the junction of Forest Road and King Edward Avenue at about 8.00 pm on the night of the murder. They had stepped into the dual carriageway and made him brake sharply. The boy had dyed punk hair, "like a pot of geraniums cropped off flat". Another youth was seen running nearby. A young couple were seen in a bus shelter in Forest Road. There was a youth pushing a motor scooter. There were several other running youths. There was a youth with a motorbike sitting on the curb opposite the Black Pad, weeping. There was a youth described as a "teddy boy" who said something offensive to a driver. Surely they were an extinct species by 1983.

One of the few who could be traced had scrawled "Lynda Mann" on a telephone directory in a kiosk. He came forward voluntarily to tell how, during a phone chat, he had talked to a friend about whether they knew the victim's family. Another was a 14 year old cyclist who rode a bike with cowhorn handlebars and derailleur gears. He had a reputation for lurking in lanes and footpaths to frighten girls and women, and he was interviewed but eventually ignored.

The police carried out a massive door to door enquiry so that by February they had taken three thousand statements. By Easter the centre at the Hospital was closed and in August the enquiry shut down. In books and on TV detectives never give up, but in real life there are priorities for manpower and money. The file had thirty possible suspects and not one probable.

****

In the months that followed the case was not forgotten. The local press kept it alive and from time to time the police issued appeals, but no fresh clues came in. Meanwhile there was other news in the county of Leicestershire. At Leicester University a researcher called Alec Jeffreys was experimenting with deoxyribonucleic acid, better known as DNA.

As everybody now knows, DNA is the chemical code pattern that defines an individual human being and which is present in human tissue and fluids.

From one person to another the huge chains of code are virtually identical, but they are normally the same only in identical twins. In others there are almost always small areas of complete distinction. Jeffreys's experiments were to find a way of identifying and highlighting those differences so that easy comparisons could be made between specimens. In the autumn of 1984 he succeeded. In 1985 he published his process, winning a professorship and academic medals, and said, "This makes me very hopeful that it will become a recognised method .. [of identification]..".

On 31st July 1986 15 year old Dawn Ashworth was working at her part time school holiday job in a Narborough newsagent's shop. At 3.30 pm she collected her wages, bought a lipstick with a gift of sweets for a neighbour's child and left for home. She had promised to be home by 7.00 pm as her mother and father were going to the child's birthday party. On the way she intended to call on friends.

She was seen by two girls passing the tennis courts and approaching a place called Ten Pound Lane, a footpath that skirted the grounds of Carlton Hayes Hospital. She had been warned after the death of Lynda Mann to avoid footpaths and stick to the road, but it was broad afternoon daylight. She cut through the lane to her friends' homes. Both were out and she left, heading back the way she had come. About 4.40 pm a motorist saw her approaching the gate to Ten Pound Lane.

At 7.00 pm her parents were ready to leave for the party but Dawn was not home. They abandoned the party and searched for her, eventually finding her two friends sitting in the village. They had not seen her. Robin and Barbara Ashworth waited until Dawn's usual curfew at 9.30, then called the police.

This time the police took the matter seriously, very seriously indeed. Early next day a large force of constables with tracker dogs searched Narborough. Soon they found a girl's denim jacket in fields by Ten Pound Lane and the motorway footbridge. The pockets contained a cigarette packet and a new lipstick. The next day they found the body of Dawn Ashworth in a field by Ten Pound Lane, covered with hay, weeds and foliage. She had been beaten, sexually assaulted and strangled. Once again the culprit had ejaculated prematurely.

****

Two hundred officers were assigned to what was now the hunt for a serial killer and the information began to accumulate. There were running youths again, there was a youth crouching in long grass close to the motorway footbridge, and many, many more.

It is no use having piles of information if you cannot find meaningful patterns. In the Lynda Mann enquiry no clear patterns had emerged but in the Dawn Ashworth case a pattern soon started to appear.

A .TEW

There was a red motorbike parked under the motorway bridge at noon on the murder day. There was a motorbike there at 4.45 pm on the same day. There was a motorcyclist in a red helmet who rode slowly up and down Mill Lane when Dawn's body was found, and the next day, slowly passed and repassed the Ashworth's house. On the first day of the search police officers saw a red helmeted motorcyclist watching them twice in three hours.

On the day after the body was found a constable was approached by a youth with a red motorcycle. He said he was a kitchen porter at Carlton Hayes Hospital and on Thursday evening had seen Dawn walking towards

59

the gate of Ten Pound Lane. A detective interviewed the youth who also reported a suspicious boy with a bike.

What seemed like a breakthrough came on 7th August. A friend of the motor cycling porter called the Incident Room to say that on 31st July he had been on holiday, but had gone to the hospital to collect his pay. The porter had called on him late the next night to say that Dawn's body had been found, in a hedge near a gate by the M1 bridge.

The kitchen porter was asked where he got his information. "Someone told me", he said, "that her body was hanging from a tree". On 8th August the porter was arrested.

At Wigston Police Station the youth was questioned for hours. This was years before the Court of Appeal recognised that repetitive questioning of even a robust and intelligent suspect can become oppressive and lead to false admissions. In a long drawn out series of interviews the boy denied the offence, then partially admitted it, then withdrew.

Other information about him emerged. Years earlier he had ridden a bike with cowhorn handlebars and had a reputation for frightening girls and women. During the Lynda Mann enquiry he had been interviewed, then discarded. He admitted to assaulting a 9 year old girl. He admitted premature ejaculation. The police became more and more certain that they had their killer. One thing he would not admit was having anything to do with the death of Lynda Mann.

He was charged with the murder of Dawn Ashworth and remanded in custody to Winson Green Prison. Superintendent Baker's team continued to detail the case against him and, in particular, to prove that he was responsible for Lynda Mann's death as well. They could not believe that little Narborough had been the scene of two such similar killings by two different murderers.

Someone, and it may have been Superintendent Baker, had heard about Alec Jeffreys's technique with DNA. It had been used in an immigration case and a paternity case. The courts seemed to be happy with DNA comparisons as evidence. Could it prove that the porter was a double killer? A blood sample from him and samples of the semen from the dead girls were sent to Leicester University.

The result of the tests were a shock. Professor Jeffreys confirmed what the police suspected, that both girls were victims of the same killer, but he also showed that the porter was not that killer. More than three months after his arrest the boy was released and the hunt began again.

★★★★★★★

While the police were preparing a case against the porter they had ignored the hundreds of messages that still came in from the public. Now they began to review them while even more arrived. One was an anonymous call about a man in Littlethorpe which offered a name. He had been interviewed in the Lynda Mann enquiry, he had previous convictions for indecent exposure and was not alibied, but had been dropped because he only moved to Narborough a month after the crime. He was ignored again.

Over Christmas the police decided on a revolutionary new approach. DNA comparison might have dealt them a severe blow but it could still be used to their advantage. On 1st January 1986 they announced that they were going to invite every male in the neighbouring villages of Narborough, Enderby and Littlethorpe who were born between 1st January 1953 and 31st December 1970, and who had no alibi, to give samples for DNA testing.

A long process began. Each volunteer had to come to a testing centre where he would be asked to prove his identity. If he had no photographic ID (and few people did then) a Polaroid picture would be taken for confirmation by people who knew him. Doctors would take blood and saliva samples. If testing did not reveal a Group A PGM 1+ secretor the test went no further. All PGM 1+'s were sent to the Home Office laboratories at Aldermaston where Professor Jeffreys's testing was now being done.

Apart from local men there were those who had left the area. They had to be visited, as did those who failed to volunteer. Miles and hours piled up, as did test phials in the laboratories, and still the testing went on.

Suddenly there was another suspect. Someone remembered an itinerant worker who had been on a pipe laying job in the area when Dawn died. A check revealed that he had left the job on the day she disappeared and flown out of the UK. He had a flight to Canada booked for two days later, but paid a Nottingham travel agent a penalty for cancelling and an additional fee for an immediate booking to California. He did not return to the job to collect nearly a thousand pounds in wages due to him.

Investigation revealed that he had been working near the Black Pad when Lynda Mann died. The man was 29, a goodlooking womaniser who had once been a disco bouncer. In Nottingham his ex wife refused to discuss his sexual preferences and habits but he was known to be violent with convictions for grievous bodily harm. The FBI were asked to trace him and acquire samples, but they failed. Leicestershire Police never found out what had driven their suspect out of Britain, but they did come to know that he was not their man, and so another lead died.

By the summer of 1987 they had tested nearly four thousand men and youths but the desperately overworked laboratories had eliminated only two thousand. Senior police management began to wind the operation down and manpower was reduced There must be a result soon or the enquiry would fall back into limbo.

On 1st August 1987 a group of bakery employees spent their lunch hour in a Leicester pub called the Clarendon. They chatted about one of their colleagues and one drinker became uneasy. She decided to talk to the policeman son of a publican she knew and phoned him, but found he was on leave. Six weeks later she rang again.

When the constable's information reached the small surviving murder team they pulled out two documents. One was a form signed by a man interviewed in the house to house enquiry about Lynda Mann; the other was the form signed by the same man when he gave his blood and saliva samples. The signatures didn't match.

Police called on Ian Kelly, a bakery worker who had been at that lunchtime session in Leicester. He quickly confessed what he had admitted to his colleagues, that he had stood in for a fellow worker at the blood test, identifying himself with a passport in which the photo had been swapped. He was arrested and charged with conspiring to pervert the course of justice.

At teatime the following afternoon the murder team finally reached their target when they arrested a colleague of Ian Kelly's in Littlethorpe and charged him with murder. He was the man whose name had been given by an anonymous caller months before, and that name was Colin Pitchfork.

✶✶✶✶✶✶✶

At a police station, Pitchfork insisted on telling his entire life story, going back to his successes as a Boy Scout and his later conviction for indecent exposure before dealing with the matters that interested the detectives. They knew about his habit of "nasty flashing" and they knew he had been an outpatient at Carlton Hayes Hospital, attending The Woodlands Day Centre. He admitted killing both Lynda Mann and Dawn Ashworth in what the police later called "a cold confession of evil".

In January 1988 Colin Pitchfork appeared at Leicester Crown Court. His DNA had been successfully matched with the specimens and he was charged with two murders, two indecent assaults, a kidnapping and with conspiracy with Ian Kelly. Kelly also appeared, charged with conspiracy, and was sentenced to eighteen months imprisonment, suspended for two years.

Pitchfork pleaded guilty to all but the kidnapping, having revealed the other offences (and the kidnapping) in his confessions to the police. He was given two life sentences for the murders, ten years for each assault and three years for conspiracy with Kelly.

✶✶✶✶✶✶✶

The case attracted worldwide attention as the first murder case in which DNA comparison was used. Now the technique, usually called "genetic fingerprinting", is commonplace in criminal trials all over the world. Even so, it is not quite the magic answer to every identification problem that many people think. Scientists regularly write reports and swear to them in court, saying that Sample A matches Sample B and that the odds against an accidental match are mathematically phenomenal. That has never been proved to be true.

In the USA criminal defenders have successfully challenged DNA evidence on several occasions, to such an extent that some years ago

British prosecutors and policemen met to consider what response they could make if the same challenges occurred in Britain. So far they have not had to worry. British defenders are far too ready to accept unscientific statements from scientists and not challenge them, but it can't be denied that Professor Jeffreys has carried criminal investigation an important stage further.

The Narborough murders deserve remembering for their place in the history of criminal investigation, but remember that DNA comparison did not identify the killer. Instead, it cleared an innocent man who had already been charged and the threat of it frightened the killer into getting himself caught by another route.

"To have been Improperly Familiar"
(Stourbridge, Worcs 1837)

A few years ago an arrested suspect stood at the Custody Sergeant's desk in a police station. Behind him stood the two arresting officers. Suddenly the prisoner was knocked senseless by a blow on the head from behind.

There were only four people in the Sergeant's office so it was certain that the blow had been struck by one of the arresting officers. Unfortunately the Sergeant had seen nothing, he had been looking down at his desk. Both arresting officers denied hitting the prisoner or seeing the other do so. Both were charged with assaulting the man and both were acquitted.

As a rule the police hate such cases. Where the evidence clearly shows that one of a small group of people committed a crime, investigators prefer to persuade one of the group to admit their guilt or to say who did it, but that doesn't always work. Then the only option is to put all the group before a court and hope that a bench of magistrates or a jury can decide who was the culprit. Sometimes they can't and the guilty one is acquitted with the innocent.

In Birmingham in the 1930s a bloodstained young man stumbled out of a house almost into the arms of a beat constable. He had been fatally stabbed. There were only two women in the house. Both were charged with his murder and both acquitted.

John Orchard, landlord of the Woolstaplers' Arms in Stourbridge, was described as being "in the prime of life and in good health". On the evening of 3rd August 1837 he walked up the yard behind his pub and into the brewhouse that stood beyond. With him went his wife, his daughter and a man named Smith.

Soon afterwards Smith returned down the yard but the Orchard family stayed in the brewhouse for some time. Only the wife and daughter emerged.

Two or three hours later John Orchard's daughter told someone at the inn that her father was ill and she was afraid he might die. A doctor was called and arrived at the Woolstaplers' Arms to find John Orchard's body seated on a chair in the pub's kitchen with Mrs Orchard supporting the head.

Mrs Orchard drew the doctor's attention to a wound in her husband's chest. Between the third and fourth ribs, immediately over the heart, was a small hole, though the doctor observed that there was no corresponding hole in Orchard's shirt. Mrs Orchard suggested that her husband had got his fatal injury by tumbling over some tubs in the yard and impaling himself on a nail. The doctor looked at the yard and noticed that yard, brewhouse and tubs seemed to have been freshly washed. It was also the doctor's opinion that Orchard had been dead at least an hour when he examined him.

At a post mortem the wound was found to be a full 4½ inches (11.5cms) deep. What is more, it had gone straight through the pericardium then the right ventricle of the heart and must have killed almost instantly.

> "Of course", says a 19th century account of the case, "grave suspicion under these circumstances could not but attach to the mother and daughter, especially as there had been repeated quarrels between them and the deceased, and the wife was also suspected to have been improperly familiar with the man Smith".

Grave suspicion or not, the Coroner's Jury baulked at naming a suspect and returned a verdict of "wilful murder against some parties unknown".

In small towns people know what is going on and talk about it. Months later a rumour spread that one of the women who had laid out Orchard's body for burial had said that he had been murdered with a skewer which was afterwards thrown into the River Stour. Questioned by the police, the woman denied ever telling such a story, but a search of the Stour produced just such a skewer as might have killed John Orchard.

Now Mrs Orchard and her daughter were arrested and charged with murder. They stood their trial at the Worcester Summer Assize in 1838, where the Judge, Lord Abinger, warned the jury that they must not convict on mere suspicion. They took this seriously and acquitted both women. No one else was ever arrested for the murder of John Orchard.

It seems to me that Mr Smith would have been at least as good a suspect as the two women. Why did he go to the brewhouse? Were he and Orchard involved in a struggle there? Is that why Orchard's shirt was off when he was stabbed? Did Smith kill his rival and then slope off, leaving the women to clear up after him and invent excuses?

Like Lord Abinger I must issue a warning. Murder cases like these are now very rare, partly through the scientific resources that are available to the police. There was a Birmingham Crown Court trial a few years ago in which more than a dozen teenagers were charged with murder. All were acquitted, but that was not because it could not be decided which one was guilty, it was because none of them could have been guilty. So, don't try and cover up a murder by hiding in a group. It probably won't work.

"The dead will rise
from their graves".
(Newent, Gloucestershire 1872)

English solicitors do not often feature as defendants in murder trials. Doctors and nurses, scientists, engineers, accountants, pilots and drivers process interminably into and out of the dock. Solicitors, though, know so well the difficulties of getting away with it, or are so skilled in concealing their crimes, that only a handful have been tried.

Two of these were Greenwood and Armstrong whose trials in the 1920s have been often written up in fact and fiction. Nearly every account of their cases comments on their profession and a coincidence. One of them practiced in Wales and the other in that strip of England that fronts onto Wales called the Marches. Strangely, there was an earlier case in the same region, so that the only three solicitors who have stood trial for capital murder in England came from the same area and for murdering their wives.

****

Edmund Edmonds preceded Greenwood and Armstrong by many years and his story is almost forgotten.

In October 1845 Edmonds married Ann Legge, widow of a man who had died in June 1844 leaving her pregnant. The child was born in October 1844 and inherited a considerable legacy from the late Mr Legge's mother. The Legge family was unhappy because they were fairly certain that Edmund and Ann had been having an affair before Legge's death, and the child was Edmonds's son.

In 1845 a blackmailer called Hollister obtained two letters written by Ann to Edmonds before their marriage which made clear that she thought Edmonds was her child's father. After some years Edmonds decided to end the blackmail and Hollister passed the letters to the Legges, who promptly sued to recover the legacy. Despite expert testimony that it was "in the highest degree improbable" that the child was sired by the departed Mr Legge, and the Judge's belief that the letters were genuine, "with the utmost reluctance" he found in favour of Edmonds.

Edmonds was free of Hollister's and the Legges's claims but he was still a professional man in a small English country town whose reputation must have been seriously damaged by the case. Even so, he carried on his practice as before.

By 1871 he was in his late fifties. The disputed child had died and four years before, so had Ann Edmonds. After her death their eldest son had emigrated to Australia. The Edmonds household consisted of Edmund, his wife's sister Mary Matthews (known as Aunt Polly), his two younger sons, Ralph and Oscar, and his niece Jeannette. She was one of seven children of Edmonds's dead brother and at 22 had lived with her uncle and helped in his office for some time.

One day while Jeannette was away from her desk Edmonds's eye fell on a letter that she had been writing. It was to "Dear Anthony", and told him that he could "have my stays made as you please".

Edmonds knew of no Anthony connected with his niece, but he did know that well-brought up young ladies did not correspond with men about their undergarments. He challenged his niece, saying, "You hussy! I have found you out!" She laughed, he slapped her face and next day she left for her mother's.

Enter Anthony, not some slim, flashing eyed subaltern who might turn a young girl's senses, but a middle aged doctor with wife and children. He had seduced Jeannette four years earlier and managed to keep the affair secret from her uncle. Anthony was Jeannette's pet name for him and hers was Cleopatra.

Having left in a hurry, Jeannette commissioned her lover to call on Edmonds to collect her heavy luggage. Edmonds and Anthony, or Dr Bass-Smith, had fallen out before, over money, and he was received coolly. Once Bass-Smith explained the reason for his call feelings heated up. "I believe you have seduced my niece, you scoundrel!" roared Edmonds. "As long as I have a feather to fly with", replied Bass-Smith, "I will have Jeannette". "I shall take good care that you do not have her long", declared Edmonds, and threw his visitor out of the house.

Bass-Smith called again and was again refused the luggage. This time he underlined his determination. If he did not get Jeannette's luggage, he declared, he would make such a stir in Newent "that the dead will rise from their graves".

Edmonds knew that this threat referred to the death of his wife, four years before, which had been in rather awkward circumstances. Bass-Smith had covered over the difficulty by signing the death certificate.

If Bass-Smith knew about the previous blackmail by Hollister he should have realised that the solicitor would not be threatened. Edmonds next issued a writ for £586.00p, money which he claimed the doctor owed him. Bass-Smith counter claimed for a large sum allegedly owed in medical fees but this failed, and rather than pay Edmonds he decided to file his petition in bankruptcy.

Edmonds announced that he would dispute the bankruptcy. Bass-Smith warned him about the rising dead again, but Edmonds went ahead and stopped the bankruptcy. Bass-Smith was now cornered. He wrote to the Coroner.

Jeannette had been staying with Bass-Smith and his wife but needed a more permanent home. A letter to the vicar of Newent resulted in him finding her a place in St James's Diocesan Home in Hammersmith, a home for "Fallen Women". Filled with Christian fervour, Jeannette wrote to her uncle asking forgiveness for her behaviour. You can judge how genuine her plea was from the fact that she also told the vicar that her uncle had murdered his wife. The vicar told the Coroner.

Coroner Carter could hardly ignore the suspicions of a clergyman and the attending doctor so he had Mrs Edmonds's body exhumed. After more than four years the result of the necropsy was inconclusive, so the Coroner held an inquiry which sat on St Valentine's Day 1872.

Inquest

Until 1898 an person accused in a criminal court could not give evidence on their own behalf, an important protection that compelled the Crown to prove its case without forcing or tricking a suspect into dubious confessions or suspicious contradictions. However, a Coroner's hearing is not a criminal proceeding and so this is the only source for Edmonds's version of events.

Edmonds said that in 1867 his wife had been experiencing the change of life and her health had been deteriorating generally. On the evening of her death he had intended to go to London, but she pressed him to stay home because she felt unwell. There had been no quarrel between them. She had gone upstairs to the room that her sister and her youngest son shared, where suddenly she said that she was dying and collapsed onto a box. Edmonds had twice gone for Dr Bass-Smith, who bled Mrs Edmonds but failed to save her life.

Edmonds said that had not struck his wife nor sworn at her, and he imagined Bass-Smith had invented the story that he had done because of the dispute over money. Questioned (as he should not have been) about whether he had an affair with his wife during her previous marriage, he called the suggestion a "gross calumny", as was a suggestion that he was having an affair with his wife's sister. Marriage to a deceased wife's sister was not allowed until 1907, and the Act which permitted it was known by its opposers as "The Poisoner's Charter".

The Coroner's Jury were not convinced by Edmonds's denials and on 16th February 1872 they found that the lady had died of apoplexy accelerated by her husband's violence. He was committed for trial on a charge of manslaughter. The Police had anticipated this result by taking him into custody the previous night.

So far things seemed to have proceeded with legal logic and order but now sleepy Gloucestershire, seeing drama on its doorstep, decided to turn it into melodrama.

On 18th February the Vicar of Newent preached a colourful sermon on the case. Whether this affected the minds of the Magistrates we don't know, but the next day Edmonds appeared before them and, on the same evidence that led a Coroner's Jury to commit him for manslaughter, he was committed to stand trial for murder. On 21st February a local farmer and maltster, James Matthews, cut his throat in an unsuccessful suicide attempt. He was the brother of Mrs Ann Edmonds and had always believed that there was something unrevealed about his sister's death.

Edmonds saw that the circus developing around his case could do him nothing but harm. He applied first for bail and second to have the case removed from Gloucestershire. Parliament had permitted the transfer of cases from one jurisdiction to another in what was called the "Palmer Act" a few years before. [See "What's your Poison?" in *Murder in the Midlands*, QuercuS (2000).] The magistrates refused bail but a judge granted it on a recognizance of £4,000 from Edmonds and up to four others in the same amount, at the discretion of the magistrates. Despite the size of the recognizances, Edmonds found his four sureties and was soon freed.

At the hearing to remove the case from Gloucestershire Edmonds's counsel argued that the Coroner was biased, that the Magistrates had no authority to commit for murder and that the Vicar's sermon, coupled with items in the local press and a piece of doggerel that was circulating locally, had so prejudiced local opinion that an unbiased jury could not be found. The Judge fudged round the Coroner's bias, side stepped the right of the Magistrates to commit for murder, censured the Vicar for his "unguarded and unfortunate" sermon and agreed that the case should go to the Old Bailey.

Trial

Gloucester Grand Jury found a true bill for murder of Mrs Ann Edmonds (formerly Legge) and on 9th May the trial opened before Baron Bramwell at the Central Criminal Court, London. Edmonds was allowed to sit with his four defending barristers rather than in the dock.

[Grand Juries in England and Wales were abolished in the 1930s but they still exist in parts of the USA. Their function was to decide whether there was enough evidence to form a case for the accused to answer. This work is now done by magistrates. Judges of the old Court of Exchequer were known as barons. This was one of three courts which were merged to form the High Court in the 1870s.]

First Witness

Ann Bradd was a servant in Edmonds's home from 1864 to 1867. She described her mistress as in good health and spirits on the day of her death. There had been friends visiting for supper and a musical evening. Mrs Edmonds had sung "Too Late! Too Late!".

Ann had gone to bed at 11 pm after the guests left, at which time Mrs Edmonds was pacing up and down the hall. The witness had heard "high words" between her master and mistress in the breakfast room and had got up to listen from the landing.

Edmonds told his wife to go to bed. She refused and called him a brute and a wretch and accused him of seeing a Miss Smallridge last time he was in Gloucester. This name, Miss Bradd said, had been mentioned over supper. She heard Edmonds say, "Damn your eyes! Go to bed!" and the sound of something heavy being thrown. The object struck something before hitting the floor and Mrs Edmonds gave a dreadful scream. Her mistress came out of the room followed by her husband. She was shouting, "There's a dear man, don't!", which she repeated three times.

72

She then went out into the garden briefly before going to her sister's room, still followed by Mr Edmonds.

Jeannette Edmonds arrived and her Aunt said, "I am dying", and asked her for some water. Ann Bradd had later seen her mistress laid on a bed with Dr Bass-Smith leaning over her. Mrs Edmonds had died shortly afterwards. She believed that the object thrown in the breakfast room was a candlestick. She also said that she had been asked twice by someone to say nothing of the candlestick incident.

Cross examined, she admitted that she had left Edmonds's service after an argument about milk. He had wanted to sack her at once but she had argued for three months notice and a reference, which she got. She had told him that he was "a bad man and that bad would be his end".

Mrs Matthews (Mrs Edmonds's mother) had questioned Ann Bradd about the death three weeks afterwards, but first Ann had pretended not to know and then said that the cause had been apoplexy. She had told the true story to a fellow servant, Anne Cassidy. Old Mrs Matthews had told Anne that it was worth "hundreds of pounds in her pocket" to say what really happened, but Ann had said she would not be bribed. She had made her prediction about Edmonds's bad end after she had given notice. It was Miss Matthews (Aunt Polly) who persuaded her to stay for three months. On leaving Edmonds had given her excellent references.

Second Witness

The virtuous, unbribable, Ann Bradd stood down, to be followed by the fallen woman in the case, Jeannette Edmonds. She said that she had been 17 when her aunt died and was educated at Edmonds's expense. She was then living in his home with Aunt Polly, 9 year old Oscar Edmonds and the servants. She remembered a major quarrel between her aunt, Anne Edmonds, and her uncle in November 1871 before the death. Mrs Edmonds had opened a letter to her husband thinking that it was addressed in a female hand. She was jealous of her husband's professional contacts with women. Jeannette had not noticed anything unusual in her uncle's attitude to Aunt Polly before his wife's death.

She remembered a row between Mrs and Mrs Edmonds early in the evening of her aunt's death, but by supper time all was calm. She had retired at about half past 10 but shortly afterwards had heard a quarrel and her aunt screaming. Jeannette had gone downstairs and seen Mrs Edmonds run out of the back dining room and go upstairs "much agitated".

She followed her into Aunt Polly's room and saw her put a candlestick on the dressing table before going to Oscar's bed. Edmonds had come in, very angry, and his wife cowered behind her son's bed saying two or three times, "Jeannette, I am dying". Her uncle said, "You be damned!" to which her aunt had replied feebly, "I won't be damned". Edmonds had rushed at his wife and punched her on the ear. Mrs Edmonds stood for a moment, asked for water, then sank down heavily on a box. Jeannette brought some water and tried to undo her aunt's dress, but could not do so because Mrs Edmonds's body "had swollen up". Edmonds moved towards his wife but Jeannette barred his way. Aunt Polly laid her sister on the floor while Jeannette sent for Dr Bass-Smith.

When the doctor arrived he asked Mrs Edmonds what she had eaten at supper. Jeannette did not tell him that her aunt had been struck. Aunt Polly and Ann Bradd were coming and going from the room while Mrs Edmonds died.

Jeannette had discussed with Aunt Polly what she had seen while still living in the house. She told Bass-Smith about it only after they had become intimate. Coroner Carter had been to see her in London and she had told him all she could remember. She did not recall seeing her uncle behave violently to his wife before the fatal occasion.

The cross examination began gently. She knew that her aunt was unwell, she had complained of pains in the head for some time and Jeannette had heard Bass-Smith say that Mrs Edmonds's heart was diseased and her death would be sudden. Jeannette's father had died in 1859 and her uncle had paid for her schooling for four years and given her a home.

Counsel now moved in on the girl's morals. She said that Bass-Smith had attempted to seduce her before her aunt died, but she had not given way until afterwards. After that intercourse had occurred regularly at her uncle's home. The doctor used to stay there as a guest and come up to her room. She knew Bass-Smith had a wife and five children. She had once spent three nights with the doctor at an inn in Kenilworth. She had not left her uncle's home because of her association with Bass-Smith.

Counsel thought that answer was a lie and went into the "Dear Anthony" episode. She said it was not the letter that made her uncle hit her, but a mistake she had made. He had hit her on the head and she said she would leave. She admitted telling the servants that she had been ordered to leave. She had not gone to the Boot Inn, Gloucester, but to a friend's house. She sent for Bass-Smith and they had gone to Gloucester and then to a friend. They had spent the night together in Leckhampton at a place where they had often spent Sunday nights. Then he took her to his home in London where his wife lived. The doctor had not practised in Newent for some time. She had left her unfinished "Dear Anthony" letter at her uncle's.

Jeannette had been admitted to the Home for Fallen Women on 22nd October and on 16th December had written to her uncle, apologising and asking his forgiveness. "The truth is my past career is bad enough without exaggeration".

She had written to her mother on 11th March, days after Mrs Edmonds' death:

> "Dear aunt appeared no worse than usual during the day; about eleven o'clock she was going to bed as usual and as was her custom went to Aunt Polly's room to talk when she was suddenly seized by apoplexy and in less than an hour had breathed her last. She was very happy after death ...... I have indeed lost my best friend."

The witness tried to discredit her own letter by saying that it was written at Aunt Polly's suggestion. She had heard that her uncle was trying to get Bass-Smith struck off the Medical Register and assumed that it was for seducing her. She had told the vicar that her uncle had killed his wife. The doctor had first seduced her when he was a guest in her uncle's home. Aunt Polly often went to bed and left Jeannette and the doctor unchaperoned, though sometimes Jeannette let him into the house. It had been her idea to contact the Vicar of Newent while she was in London.

Third Witness
The soiled blossom fluttered from the witness box to be replaced by Anthony - Dr Matthew Bass-Smith. He must have appeared to the jury as a Victorian nightmare come true, a seemingly respectable professional man who would take advantage of another man's hospitality to seduce a

girl in the household. At the inquest he had been ordered from the court and his evidence refused by the Coroner, so public and jury were agog to hear what he said now.

He said that he had been a doctor in Newent but now had no practice. He remembered Edmonds calling to say his wife had had a fit. The doctor had been dressing when Edmonds arrived again, saying that if Bass-Smith did not hurry the woman would be dead. When he arrived Mrs Edmonds was unconscious. He had tried to bleed her, applied a mustard plaster to her neck and hot water to her feet, but she had not rallied and died about three quarters after midnight.

In Edmonds's presence Bass-Smith had asked Miss Matthews if there had been any violence, because the death seemed sudden to him, but she said there had been no disturbance or violence. He had certified the cause of death as apoplexy.

A punch on the ear might cause apoplexy. Screaming and asking for water might indicate concussion. A blow might provoke apoplexy in someone who was predisposed to it. Mrs Ann Edmonds was not in the best of health and might have succumbed to any excitement.

Dr Bass-Smith had spoken with Edmonds after the funeral. The lawyer was very depressed and had admitted that he might have killed his wife by his unkindness; she had not been a good woman, he said, but he wished they might have their time again. Bass-Smith (who, of course, knew all about moral virtue) said that Mrs Edmonds had been a good woman and Edmonds's loss was her gain. Edmonds added that he had been "a brute and a villain" to his wife.

Under cross examination Bass-Smith had to admit his moral lapses. In 1867, as a married man living with his wife and four children, he had often stayed with Edmonds and had tried to seduce Jeannette. He could not recall whether this was before or after Mrs Edmonds's death. He had gone for Jeannette's luggage because she asked him to. He knew Edmonds was trying to get him struck off the Medical Register. He had not made the remark about the dead rising from their graves. He had frequent immoral relations with Jeannette and once spent three nights with her in Kenilworth. The Edmonds family said they were never happy except when he was with them.

The Doctors

The medical evidence could not rest upon such a dubious opinion as that of Bass-Smith and Dr Wilton, Senior Surgeon at Gloucester Infirmary gave evidence. He said that Mrs Edmonds's remains had been too decomposed to reach any conclusion. If the evidence he had heard was true, he would say that death arose from apoplexy induced by a blow, but the lady might have died from natural apoplexy. Her appearance was consistent with either.

Dr Wilton was followed by Dr Charlton of Gloucester, who also found no evidence in the remains to help him reach a judgement. On that uncertain note the Crown closed its case.

Mr Huddleston, counsel for the defence, began with an attack on the lovers, Bass Smith who knew that all the indications were of natural death, and Jeannette who had invented details to add verisimilitude to her lover's story. He would call Miss Matthews, whose character they had tried to blacken, but who could give them the lie.

Last Witness

Mary Matthews (Aunt Polly) was 40 and had lived with her sister's family for twelve years, taking on management of the household after her sister's death. Edmonds had been an affectionate and generous husband. There had been no quarrel and no screams that she had heard on 24th February, nor had any woman been praised for her beauty at the supper table. She had gone to bed after Jeannette, to the room she shared with her nephew Oscar. Downstairs were Mr and Mrs Edmonds with Edmonds's articled clerk, Mr Palmer. Mrs Edmonds had come to Aunt Polly's room on her way to bed and collapsed. Mrs Matthews went over the efforts made to save her. She withstood cross examination and probably made a good impression.

At this point in a modern trial the prosecution, the public and the tabloid press would be waiting for the defendant to give evidence, but it was to be a quarter of a century before those accused were allowed to give evidence in their own defence.

So the jury had heard all the evidence. There was the blackmailing doctor who deceived his wife, his family, his friend and host, and seduced his friend's niece under her uncle's roof. Then they heard the story of a rebellious girl who resented her uncle's authority, was besotted with her medical seducer and who came to the witness box fresh from a home for fallen women to be contradicted by her own letter. The jury also had the account of a servant with a suspiciously detailed memory who admitted to dealings with someone interested in convicting Edmonds as well as the evidence of two doctors who seemed to be facing both ways.

Perhaps it is not surprising that Edmund Edmonds was acquitted. Once again he had stood firm against blackmail and won the decision of a court. Whatever suspicion may have clung to him, he returned to Newent to practice law.

So Anthony and Cleopatra left the stage and the curtain fell on this production. What became of the amorous doctor and his fallen victim we do not know.

"A man of similar personality and lifestyle"
(Hereford, 1977)

Dorothy Margaret Davies was last seen alive at around 9.35 on the evening of 21st January 1977. At about 2.30 pm on Sunday the 23rd Lesley Davies, her 16 year old daughter, was dropped off near 76 Whittern Way by her grandfather. Getting no response to the doorbell and seeing that the upstairs and downstairs curtains were still drawn, she used her key. It was in the main upstairs front bedroom that she found her mother's body.

****

Harold Williams

Born in Hereford in 1933, he was the oldest of five children. His National Service was largely with the Military Police, though at this time he suffered from fainting and blackouts and was treated for *petit mal*, a type of eplilepsy

He married in 1953 and left the Army in 1955. His adultery ended the marriage 1968, but in 1969 he married again, adopting his wife's existing daughter. His new wife already had one child by him and expected another. A third child (a boy) was accidentally drowned in 1972, which affected Williams deeply. He used to visit the grave every week.

In 1973 Harold Williams was again divorced but the couple soon remarried. It was said that there were "frequent violent arguments", including one where Williams hit his wife on the head with a dinner plate causing a wound needing ten stitches. According to his wife he once tried to strangle her with a headscarf and she nearly lost consciousness. After he cut his wife's face with a carving knife he was again divorced in 1975. Deciding to have no further contact with his children, he went to live with his parents.

Williams had been long distance lorry driver but then became a coach driver. In October 1976 he was involved in an incident with a female stripper who boarded his coachful of policemen when Williams became abusive and had to be restrained. They thought that he had been drinking.

In April 1977 he was sacked after refusing to let schoolchildren shelter from the rain on his coach. He was said to have abused the organiser, made obscene gestures in front of the children and abandoned a group of late passengers. Again, it was said that he had been drinking.

In December 1975 he was introduced to Margaret Davies by a former boyfriend of hers. He moved in with her, describing himself (because she was involved in a divorce) as her "lodger". In fact they lived together, though Williams sometimes returned briefly to his parents' home.

Williams later told police that Margaret Davies had asked him to tie her hands and feet to the bed corners during intercourse, which he did on two occasions, claiming that he didn't particularly enjoy it. Former friends of Williams said that he had joined them in "threesomes", he and his friend photographing each other having sex with the friend's wife.

His years as a driver gave him a record of motoring offences but he had only one offence of violence. In December 1974 he was convicted of assault on his then wife and possessing an offensive weapon. He was fined and sentenced to three months gaol, suspended for one year.

Dorothy Margaret Davies
The woman and victim in this case was born in 1936 at Stoke on Trent. Her parents moved to Hereford, separating when she was 10. She was bright and when she left school she got a good secretarial job.

In 1958 she married the director of a computer company, by whom she had three children. He was often away from home and by the mid 1960s, the marriage deteriorated. She suspected her husband of having an affair, which was confirmed when he and his mistress were involved in a road accident. Mrs Davies began affairs of her own.

From 1967 she had treatment for depression and alcoholism. She made five suicide attempts between 1967 and 1975 and, after separation from her husband in 1973, she could not handle her children. They were placed with their grandparents who were later given custody.

Mrs Davies had a number of affairs with men, mostly short because of her drink problem. She was described as "desperate for friendship" and offered sex to keep the friendship of men.

After her mother's death in 1975 she became very isolated. It was then that she met Williams. She had been living in her former matrimonial home but moved to 76 Whittern Way, Tupsley, Hereford. Unfortunately, No 76 was almost opposite the flat where lived Margaret Williams, Williams's second ex-wife.

Trouble and Strife

With their personalities and past lives it was unlikely that Harold Williams and Margaret Davies would live happily together. Between 6th April and 18th December 1976 she made sixteen recorded complaints to the Police alleging assault and/or theft by Williams. The police thought her unreliable and likely to refuse to make a statement, so they took no action.

At about 02.55 on 3rd January 1977 police were called by Mrs Davies who complained of assault. She had a bruised, swollen left cheek and was distressed. She said Williams had got upset over his suspicion that she had been out with another man and had punched and kicked her while she was phoning a friend. He denied it, swore at Mrs Davies and went to hit her. When a PC intervened Williams took him by the lapels, shook him and pushed him onto a bed. He was arrested. Being taken outside he said, "If she carries on like this, I'll kill the ****!"

He said that he had hit her on the left cheek after she had been moaning at him. He denied more than one blow and kicking her but was charged with assault. On 4th January Hereford City Magistrates bailed him on condition that he lived with his mother and had no contact with Mrs Davies.

On 18th January Williams pleaded guilty to the assault and the case was adjourned for psychiatric reports, with bail extended to 15th February 1977.

Dr Annesley told the Court that in his view Williams was a smooth, obsequious individual with a vicious temper. ECG examination had shown no abnormality, Williams was not suffering from any mental illness and could be considered fully responsible for his actions.

Later police enquiries showed that Williams continued to hang about near Mrs Davies' home. On 8th January 1977 two of her neighbours saw him driving slowly along Whittern Way looking towards her house. They told her and she stayed the night at their home. Next day neighbours escorted her home from the White House Inn on Whittern Way. She told them she had just seen Williams drive past her, turn and repass, and she was frightened.

On 16th January Williams called on friends off Whittern Way, but the husband was out and his wife refused to admit Williams.

Between 17th and 21st January Williams drove a Golden Valley school coach which passed along Whittern Way twice daily. One stop was outside No. 76. A child said that on 19th January Williams got out at the Whittern Way stop and announced that he was going in for a cup of tea. There was no cafe nearby. Another witness said that a Golden Valley coach was parked in Whittern Way sometime between 10.00 am and 3.00 pm on 21st January. No other Golden Valley driver went there on that day. Mrs Davies had contacted Golden Valley at 12.50 trying to speak to Williams about a business matter.

It was at about 2.30 pm on Sunday 23rd January 1977 that Lesley Davies found her mother's body and phoned her grandparents

Inquest

Home Office pathologist, Dr Davis, examined Mrs Davies and found rigor mortis fully developed and the beginning of putrefaction. Fresh bruises appeared on her left leg. Immediately above the Adam's apple was a narrow ligature mark with a slight overlap and a small gap at the back of the neck. On the left there was a little bruising around the ligature mark and faint abrasions, suggesting that she had tried to remove the ligature.

Mrs Davies had six stab wounds in and just below her left breast. One had passed through the third rib and penetrated her lung, showing that the knife had been driven with some force. Two of these strikes had pierced only subcutaneous fat, but three had penetrated the woman's chest cavity. She had four puncture wounds in her neck and upper chest, made with a "bodkin-like" implement. Dr Davis thought that all the wounds were inflicted after death. He found no evidence of sexual interference.

Davis believed that the stab and puncture wounds could have been caused by a knife and a knitting needle later found in Williams's car. He certified the cause of death as ligature strangulation and the time of death about two days before he saw the body, that is, on Friday 21st January.

Questions, questions
It was quite obvious that the police would suspect the man who had recently been charged with assaulting Mrs Davies and at 6.30 pm on Sunday 23rd January 1977 they went to Williams's home.

At first they did not tell him why they were there. They asked when he last saw Mrs Davies and he said, "Not since I was put on bail. Well, you know I'm not allowed to go and see her. She's been ringing me up at work but I've had nothing to do with her". He produced a note that on 20th January she had phoned work and left a message for Williams to ring her. Williams said, "I didn't ring her, but I made a note to show she keeps trying to contact me". He also showed a list of decorating jobs he had carried out for Mrs Davies, saying that she had been trying to contact him because she was short of money and wanted him to pay her bills.

Told that she was dead, he broke into tears. After recovering he said, "You know, you might not believe it, but I really loved that girl. There are only two people I have really loved and that's my son who you know drowned, and her. How did she die? Was she on the bed?"

Williams blamed Mrs Davies's GP for her death on account of tablets he had prescribed, adding that she was a lovely woman at times but that in drink she was a bitch. She had threatened to dig up his son's grave.

Williams went voluntarily to the Police Station. While waiting there he was seen to be picking at the quick of a fingernail making it bleed, then dabbed the blood with a handkerchief. Told that Mrs Davies had been murdered he repeated, with great emphasis, that he hadn't seen her or contacted her since his bail.

Williams was questioned again on 24th January and asked to account for his movements on 21st January. He said that after work, wearing a sports jacket and brown trousers, he had visited a pub from 5.30 to 6.00 pm with a friend, Marshall Griffiths. With another friend, Phillip Powell, he ate at the City Walls steak bar, leaving at about 10.45pm. Powell later said Williams had drunk four or five ciders and some wine and was not drunk but "fairly merry". Leaving his friends, Williams had gone to the Friar Tuck chip shop and bought fish and chips, then bought more fish and chips in Grandstand Road. He went home and to bed at about half past midnight on Saturday 22nd January.

Questioned again later the same day, he was told that Griffiths had said that they had met at 6.30 pm on Friday. He said that he was confused, but that he knew in his own mind that he was not guilty. He was given five minutes to sort out his thoughts but said that he still couldn't think.

A detective then told him that their enquiries showed that he was not at the Grandstand Road chip shop (where he was well known) on Friday evening. He insisted that he had been there. His police questioner accused Williams of lying and it was said that he went red in the face and looked uncomfortable. He refused to answer further questions until a solicitor was present.

Williams owned a semi derelict car, apart from the one which he drove. For reasons never explained the Police kept it under surveillance. On 27th January he was seen to go to this car and spend about fifteen minutes at the boot. In a later interview he is said to have agreed that he went to the car, but said that he put nothing in and took nothing from it.

Arrest

On 18th February Williams was arrested and asked about a pair of light brown trousers which the police had taken from his home. He said that they had been dry cleaned. Asked about letters and a diary belonging to Mrs Davies found in his current car, he refused to answer.

On 19th February Williams was told that Revd. Hall Matthews had said Williams told him that he would rather kill Mrs Davies than let anyone else have her. He was reminded of his threat against her on 3rd January. He did not remember saying this to Hall Matthews, adding that he had said a lot of things to Mrs Davies which should not be taken too seriously. He denied breaking bail. He was told that an Anglia car, like his, had been seen parked near Whittern Way between 6.30 and 7.00 pm on 21st January. He said it was not his and he had no reason to drive along Whittern Way to go home from work.

Williams agreed that he might have met Griffiths later than he first thought on 21st January as he might have gone home first. Asked to describe the serving staff in the Grandstand Road chip shop, he described people who hadn't been there that day.

The police put it to him that the Friar Tuck chip shop was half a mile from his home, whereas the Grandstand Road shop took him a mile and a half out of his way. This was a route that only made sense if he wanted to get to Whittern Way. Williams said it might seem strange to buy further chips after two meals, but it was true and he had not gone to Whittern Way.

Williams's mother had told the police that her son returned home about half past midnight on 22nd January and left for work at 8.00 am on the same day, but Police had evidence suggesting that he had not spent the night at home. Three witnesses said that his car was not in its usual position outside his home at 12.30 am, 2.30 am or 4.30 am on 22nd January. Williams said they were all mistaken.

His employer, Mr Crockett, had said he had found Williams asleep in his car at Crockett's yard at 7.45 am, with the engine running. Williams said that he had only arrived just before Crockett and was not asleep.

The discrepancies in his account of his movements and the stories of him being seen around Whittern Way in January were put to him, but he did not comment on either.

The police told Williams that an impression in blood on Mrs Davies's body bore a "close resemblance" to the weave pattern of his light brown trousers, and that a witness saw him in light brown trousers on 21st January. A burn in the trousers, they said, could have come from a dropped cigarette while he was asleep in his car on 21st January. Williams said that he was wearing dark brown trousers on 21st January and that he burnt them while working on his coach.

The police told him of "other blood", apart from his, on his handkerchief, but couldn't account for it.

Evidence

On 21st February the police officers involved recited to Harold Williams the factors which they thought showed that he had killed Margaret Davies

(1) That Mrs Davies's private papers and address book were found in Williams's car, and the evidence of a folder and her handbag being searched by someone who knew the whereabouts of such items.

(2) Williams's claim to have received a number of phone calls from her, but only recorded one on 20th January, meaning 21st January.

(3) His list of coach driving jobs, kept as though he was expecting the Police to call.

(4) The knots Williams had used to tie raspberry canes for an ex-girlfriend were similar to those used on Mrs Davies.

(5) A magazine found in his bedroom had a drawing of a gagged, bound, woman, similar to the way Mrs Davies was bound.

(6) Williams had said that he had gone to bed on the afternoon of 22nd January and shaved when he got up, suggesting that he had not been home the previous night and had not had much sleep

(7) Mrs Davies's murderer entered her home without breaking in. Since she had phoned Williams, she would have let him in to settle her bills.

(8) He had lied about his movements after 11.30 on 21st January.

This all seems to suggest a fairly weak case, unless the police intended to charge Williams with stalking, which was not an offence at that time.

Williams replied to all this that he was innocent and that he had not been to Mrs Davies's house after being bailed. He was bailed once more by the police.

After this month of repeated questioning, Harold Williams must have expected more of the same, but suddenly it stopped. The police did not interview him again until 13th April, when they asked how Mrs Davies had come to ring Oakley's Transport on 16th January about Williams, when it was the day before he applied for a job there and he had not been in contact with her. He said that Mrs Davies had a knack of finding things out if she wanted to.

On 13th January he had given pots of jam to two women in a pub, jam that had come from the same batch as the jam found in Mrs Davies' home. He said that he had taken the jam from Mrs Davies' home about Christmas 1976.

The next day the police asked Williams about his clothing on 21st January. His sister, they said, remembered him wearing a check jacket and light brown trousers at lunchtime on that day. Phillip Powell thought Williams had worn cream to light brown trousers and Mr Crockett said that Williams was wearing his check jacket when he saw him in his car on the morning of 22nd January. Williams said all three were mistaken, that he was wearing his working uniform (black blazer and grey flannels) when Crockett found him.

Williams had collected a party of Irish farriers from the Lichfield Hotel, Hereford on 22nd January, and he was in working uniform. However, a phone caller to the Hotel at 7.50 am had warned the party to be ready at 8.20. It was suggested that he had made the call to give himself time to go home and change.

Williams denied making the call or returning home to change. He said that the light brown trousers were last dry cleaned on 11th January, but on 23rd January police noticed that they seemed to have been "recently" wet washed and freshly ironed. He said that this was not so.

The police next produced a paper which Williams had given them on 23rd January listing men associated with Mrs Davies, and asked when he had written it. He said it was before they first saw him about the murder, that it was because he felt it was wrong that he was the only corespondent named in Mrs Davies's divorce. He said that a spot of blood on its back might be from when he picked his fingers after being taken to the police station for the first time. He had not been observed to pick his fingers at any other time and police suspected he had done it to explain "other blood" (which could not be grouped) on his handkerchief.

It seems that after this interview Williams was released without bail, which might lead us to think that the police were recognising the weakness of their case.

Once more, there was no more questioning until 2nd June 1977 when Williams was again arrested. "What, again?" he said. "You've dropped a fucking bollock here. It's taken you bloody long enough, nearly six months!" He was charged with the murder of Margaret Davies.

Trial
The police had taken more than 1,600 statements of which some were second or third interviews with the same witness. In preparing for the trial the junior barrister for Williams, Mr Dixon, had to read not only the witness statements put forward as part of the Crown's case but also all the others. At least three statements were not revealed to him. They had been

made by a Mrs Emily Williams and it seems that they were withheld on the advice of the Crown's Leading Counsel, a blatant breach of his obligations to the defence.

Many of the statements were about men who were acquainted with Margaret Davies, some of them married. There was masses of gossip about Williams and Mrs Davies. For example, Williams had told many people that he would kill Mrs Davies. He had also told people that she was a "nympho" and could only be "got going" if tied up.

Mr Dixon noted an enormous number of men who had sexual relations with Margaret Davies, and that some names and phone numbers in her diary were those of men who claimed not to have met her or even heard of her.

When Williams came to trial at Hereford Crown Court the police pathologist, Dr Davis, had changed his tune. Having said at first that death occurred about forty eight hours before discovery of Mrs Davies's body (on Friday afternoon), he had realised that Margaret Davies had been seen after that and so changed his opinion to death late on Friday night. He was sure that she had died of strangulation, despite the fact that petecchiae (the small blood-spots around the eyes that appear in strangulation) were not present. He suggested that a round tipped tableknife found in Williams's possession was the stabbing implement and that the piercing wounds were made with a steel knitting needle, one of which was found in Williams's car. He was positive that the victim died before the various wounds were inflicted.

Williams had explained the knitting needle as one of the things he used when fishing for eels. The Crown called a TV fishing "expert" to say that he had never heard of a knitting needle being used in catching eels.

There was evidence of a large diary/address book missing from Margaret Davies's home, but it was not found in Williams's possession.

Probably the worst part of the case against Williams was the part he constructed himself, his transparent lies about his Friday night movements. Whatever the reason, he was convicted and sentenced to the mandatory sentence of life imprisonment with no recommendation as to its minimum length.

Had he been prepared to accept the verdict, Williams might have been released on parole in eight years or so, but he maintained his innocence and thereby fell into the "Catch 22" which the Parole Board operates. The Board insists that it does not penalise prisoners who insist on their innocence, on the other hand it refuses parole to those who "fail to address their wrongdoing".

So Harry Williams stayed in prison and the years passed. Then in 2000, at the age of 67, his MEP referred the case to the newly created Criminal Cases Review Board and the Board referred it to the Court of Appeal. Williams was granted Legal Aid and a solicitor began to prepare an appeal. It soon became clear that there were many things wrong with the case.

The medical evidence was a mess. Dr Davis, who was later sacked for incompetence, failed even to note whether Mrs Davies had an appendix (an important factor in post-mortem putrefaction). He cheerfully suggested death by strangling with a ligature without significant petechiae being found in the body to justify that conclusion. He thought that wounds were inflicted after death, though they were bleeding which would indicate the contrary. He accepted without comment that the blunt, round tipped table knife was the stabbing weapon. His evidence as to time of death was worthless.

The killer's search of Mrs Davies's handbag suggested a married man other than Williams who was widely known to associate with her.

The unpointed table knife was a most unlikely stabbing weapon. Flesh and skin are elastic and resist pressure. A blunt weapon usually has to be twisted to break the skin and should leave a characteristic wound.

The question arose of the three statements that the defence never saw. It turned out that they were from Margaret Williams, Harold's former wife. This lady (who is long dead) insisted that she had a cup of tea with Margaret Davies on Saturday 22nd January 1977, the day after Dr Davis insisted she was killed, but the documents have disappeared.

There was other suppressed evidence. One man had confessed to the crime. The police simply told the defence that the man was mad and never supplied his statement.

It seemed possible that Harold Williams could present a good case to the Court of Appeal and might well be released. The press pointed out that he was the longest serving "miscarriage of justice" convict in Britain.

It did not happen. As his case was being made ready to present, Harold Williams died in prison having spent more than twenty years inside. His family tried to obtain a decision that he had been wrongfully convicted, but their action failed in 2003. For all official purposes, Harold Williams remains the murderer of Margaret Davies.

And was he? Well, he seems to have lied and lied about his movements on the Friday night, but that doesn't make him a killer. Who knows his reasons for not telling the truth? The police were satisfied that he was a violent man who assaulted women, and so he was, but he was a sentimental, mouthy drunk, who shouted and struck out in anger or drink. The murder of Margaret Davies was more coldblooded. The wounds were almost certainly inflicted before death, and Margaret died of strangulation from the gag or vagal inhibition. The vagus nerve controls the heart rate and it can be shut down by shock or sexual excitement. The table knife and the knitting needle were most unlikely weapons, and, incidentally, knitting needles can be used in catching eels, as books on angling show.

There was no evidence that Williams was excited by bondage, and there was a prime piece of evidence that the killer was not Williams - the scattered papers, the rifled handbag and the missing diary/address book. That was the work of a man who wanted to leave no trace of his identity at the scene. For Williams that would have been pointless. The police knew about his association with the dead woman, but what about those men who couldn't account for their names being in her address book? To one of those, particularly a married man, finding the address book and destroying it would have been vital.

What of the long gaps the police left in questioning Williams? What was going on then? Part of the time the police may have been investigating the second suspect, for there was one. He is described by the police as a man "of similar personality and lifestyle" to Williams, but a married man. He drove a distinctive vehicle and that vehicle was seen outside the murder house late on 21st January. Unlike Williams, he refused to answer questions or make a statement. His movements on the Friday night were sworn to by his wife and so, with only one suspect left, the police fell back on Harry Williams. The statements dealing with the investigation of this man were denied to Williams's defence.

It may be that Harold Williams did murder Margaret Davies, or it may be that the second suspect succeeded in murdering her and destroying Williams's life without any penalty.

"If Police or tricks, death."
(Highley, Shropshire 1975)

Donald Skepper, son of a Yorkshire subpostmaster, woke on 15th February 1974 to a nightmare. A masked man holding a shotgun was demanding the keys to the post office safe. Not finding them where Donald had said they would be, the robber woke the boy's parents and repeated the demand. Donald shouted, "Let's get him!", and was shot dead. The masked intruder escaped.

The murder of Donald Skepper was the first killing by a man who was already causing concern to the police. For more than six years the killer had robbed, mainly subpost offices, nearly always using the same method. In the small hours he would drill through a window frame, release the catch and climb in. The sleeping residents would be wakened to face his shotgun and a demand for keys. The robber was always dressed in the same way: military camouflage clothing, black plimsolls, white gloves and a black hood. He had stolen more than £20,000 before he began killing.

Seven months after the murder of Donald Skepper, on 6th September, subpostmaster Derek Astin of Higher Baxenden, Lancs, grappled with a masked robber. He was shot dead in front of his wife and children.

These two killings seem to have made the North of England too hot for the murdering thief and now he moved to the Midlands. In November 1974 he attacked the post office at Langley, Worcestershire, where he fracturing the skull of Margaret Greyland and shot dead her postmaster husband, Sidney, for £800.

Up to this point the story of the thefts and killings had been largely ignored by the national media but events would soon make the killer the most wanted man in Britain. His nickname, "The Black Panther", became familiar to every newspaper reader and television watcher.

Kidnap

On 14th January 1975, less than a year after the first killing, Dorothy Whittle woke in her home at Highley, Shropshire, to find that her pretty 17 year old daughter, Lesley, had vanished during the night. Messages stamped onto Dymotape had been left which established that the girl had been kidnapped from her bed. The tapes demanded £50,000 and set out conditions: "No police...you are on a time limit. If police or tricks, death".

Cold blooded kidnapping for ransom is rare in Britain. A century ago it was the speciality of mountain bandits in Southern Europe and the Mediterranean countries who preyed profitably on wealthy travellers. W.S.Gilbert, lyric writer of the Gilbert & Sullivan operettas, was kidnapped as a child. When little Charley Ross was stolen from his wealthy parents' lawn in Philadelphia in the 1880s, America was outraged because such a crime was unknown there, but times change and kidnapping has become universal.

All kidnappers demand no contact between the family and the police. Some victims are stupid enough to agree but it rarely does any good. The Whittle family, who owned a successful coaching firm, did not hesitate and Lesley's elder brother, Ronald Whittle, contacted West Mercia Police.

As kidnapping has become more common in Britain police forces have developed techniques to deal with it. One is to ask the media to maintain silence until the issue can be resolved, but for some reason West Mercia did not do this. When the story reached the BBC it was broadcast the same evening as a newsflash. That broadcast has been blamed for aborting a first attempt to receive a phone message from the kidnapper.

As the police waited in vain for a contact, a different drama was played out in another part of the Midlands. Security guard Gerald Smith was making a routine patrol of the big Freightliner container depot at Dudley when he noted a man loitering about the perimeter fence. His furtive manner worried Smith and he decided to call the police. As he turned from the fence he was shot in the back six times.

Despite his terrible injuries (which caused his death fourteen months later) Smith bravely crawled to a phone and called the police. Examination of the crime scene showed that the Black Panther had been at work. Cartridges ejected from the gun that injured Gerald Smith bore ejection scars identical to those left at two previous robberies. The loiterer at the Freightliner depot had used a green Morris 1300 car and its discovery provided more evidence. The car contained Dymotape messages similar to those left at Lesley Whittle's home and which were evidently meant to be part of a series of instructions on the delivery of the ransom. It also contained a cassette with a recording of a message from Lesley to her mother.

Gerald Smith was able to provide a description of the intruder, and a portrait based on it was quickly circulated to all media.

A corner of Bathpool Park.

Bathpool Park

Late on the following night (16th January) Ronald Whittle took a phone call from the kidnapper. Arrangements were made for Ronald to deliver the ransom and he set out with the money and a covert police escort to follow a complicated trail of directions. They led him at last to Bathpool Park near Kidsgrove, Staffordshire, a large area of woodland and open space. There he was supposed to flash his headlights and await a response from the kidnapper with a torch.

Ronald Whittle flashed his headlights in Bathpool Park but there was no answering signal.

The kidnapper was later to say that he was at the rendezvous that night but was frightened by the sudden appearance of a marked police patrol car in the Park, so he dropped the arrangement. The West Mercia Police group following Ronald's journey were not using marked cars, but Bathpool Park lies in the area of Staffordshire Police. They have always insisted that they had no marked car in Bathpool Park that night. Even so, a courting couple insist that they saw a marked Staffordshire Police car that night close to the rendezvous site.

Police forces are highly protective of their patches; they do not care to have other forces at work there, even less so when the crime is a high profile one and any capture will bring national headlines. Did Staffordshire Police give someone a watching brief to keep an eye on West Mercia's operations? Did some officers decide to try the Park so that West Mercia shouldn't take all the glory? Was the patrol in the Park a pure accident? It seems certain that there was a marked car in Bathpool Park that night and equally certain that we shall never know why. What also seems certain is that the presence of that car led directly to the aborting of the ransom attempt and failure to catch the kidnapper, and to the death of Lesley Whittle.

****

Because of the complexity and importance of the Black Panther investigation, Scotland Yard were called in to help the provincial forces of the North and the Midlands with their superior facilities and expertise. The Yard now demonstrated its expertise by organizing a search of Bathpool Park. It found nothing of any significance, nor did they notice that beneath the Park lies a complex of concrete chambers and tunnels which are part of a drainage system.

Local children playing in the Park were more successful. They found a Dymotape strip with the message, "Drop suitcase into hole'" and a torch wedged into the grille over a ventilation shaft to the tunnel system.

When a head teacher handed these items to the police a second search of the Park was organized, this time with tracker dogs and including a search of the subterranean complex. The underground search had not gone far before they found the body of Lesley Whittle, naked and hanging by its neck from a noose of wire shackled to an iron access ladder. Nearby was other evidence that this was where the kidnapper had kept his prisoner.

After discovery of the teenager's body there were recriminations among the police forces and changes in the investigation team. Even so, as the year moved on the Black Panther was ever present in the news media and the police seemed no nearer to catching him.

The enormous police task force moved about the Midlands and the North of England following the slenderest leads. A former teacher had no convictions but had successfully sued his former head teacher for alleging that the teacher had an improper relationship with a girl pupil. He returned one night to his country home to find the lights on, the door open and police officers waiting to question him about Lesley Whittle. Two West Midland contractors working in North Wales were arrested by a coachload of police as they left a village pub one night and held overnight. A fellow drinker had seen a television item about the Panther and decided that one of the strangers in the bar might be the killer.

The police knew that their quarry was wily and devious, ruthless, cowardly and nervous, and that his cowardice led him to kill instantly when it was not warranted. They did not know how to catch him.

Arrest

It was 11th December 1975, eleven months after the kidnapping and killing of Lesley Whittle, when fortune finally smiled on the police. Two Nottinghamshire officers, PCs Stuart Mackenzie and Tony White, were on a routine panda car patrol of the village of Mansfield Woodhouse when they spotted a small, dark man with a holdall who seemed to behave furtively. Challenged by the officers, the suspect produced a sawn off shotgun and forced them back into their car.

With White in the back and Mackenzie in the driver's seat, the suspect slipped into the front passenger seat. Jamming the shotgun against Mackenzie's ribs, he commanded, "Drive!"

The constable obeyed but had no intention of leaving their passenger with the upper hand. In a series of silent messages, conveyed by glances at the rear view mirror, he indicated his intentions to PC White so that he would be ready for action.

As the panda car came to a T-junction, Mackenzie stamped hard on the brake, bringing the car to a shuddering halt and throwing the intruder off balance. With the gun no longer pointed at his partner, White grabbed for it. There was a struggle in which the shotgun fired. White's hand was hit and Mackenzie's eardrums were perforated by the blast, but they clung on.

The car had stopped close to a late night chip shop and a customer saw the struggle spill out of the smoking car. He went to help the officers and together they restrained and arrested the gunman. White and Mackenzie did not know it, but good routine police work backed by courage and enterprise and some public help had succeeded where a massive task force had failed. They had arrested the Black Panther.

****

The man they had arrested turned out to be Donald Neilson, born in Bradford in 1936. Originally called Donald Nappey, he had changed his name to avoid the inevitable jokes. Neilson had done his National Service with the Army in Cyprus during the emergency and had become obsessed with techniques of guerrilla warfare and survival. A search of his Bradford home revealed plenty of evidence against him, including a quantity of ex Army equipment and, oddly enough, a small statue of a black panther.

Tried on four counts of murder and one of kidnapping, Neilson insisted that the death of Lesley Whittle had been an accident. He had fully intended to accept the ransom from Ronald Whittle, he said, and later release the girl. After taking her he had established a hideout in the underground complex at Kidsgrove. There he had made a prisoner of Lesley by taking away her clothes and securing her to the access ladder with the wire noose. Alongside the ladder was a horizontal grilled platform, on which the girl had spent her time.

On the night of 16th January, as Ronald Whittle followed the trail of clues to Bathpool Park, Neilson had waited for him. Suddenly he saw a marked police car prowling about the Park. Afraid that the police had set a trap for him, he scurried back to the drain tunnels and clambered down the ladder. As he dropped onto the grill platform he had bumped against Lesley, who lost her balance and fell from the platform, being killed instantly by the wire noose about her neck. His story certainly makes sense since at that point Neilson had no conceivable reason to kill the girl, added to which, Detective Superintendent Booth of Mercia Police gave evidence of the panda car debacle at Bathpool.

Whether his story was true or not, the jury convicted him of all four murders and the kidnapping. He was sentenced to four life sentences and sixty one years in prison, where he remains.

Nielson's last victim was not the subject of a murder charge. Murder in English law occurs when death follows within a year and a day of the fatal act. Gerald Smith, the courageous security guard at the Dudley Freightliner depot, died of his injuries in March 1976, fourteen months after he was shot by the Black Panther.

SHOCKING BARBARITY AT WEST BROMWICH

"Attended with terrible cruelty"
(West Bromwich, Staffs, 1871)

"About half past five on Sunday morning", wrote the *Illustrated Police News* of 8th July 1871, "a supposed murder, attended with terrible cruelty, was discovered at the Hall End Pits, belonging to Mr Alford, at Church Lane, West Bromwich".

An engine tender called Isaac Blocksidge had gone to a shack on the pit bank to wake a man known as Lame Joe Marshall, an elderly cripple.

> "The old man was on the ground at the front of a large fire, from which he was separated only by a few feet, and his right side was covered with fire, which apparently had been taken from the fireplace for the purpose and his flesh was literally being roasted".

Blocksidge dashed water on the flames but old Joe was dead. Apart from terrible burns he had several holes in his head which seemed to have been inflicted with a hammer or two rakes which were in the hovel. It was supposed that, having beaten the old man to death, the killer had tried to destroy his body by fire.

After putting out the fire Blocksidge ran to a nearby lodging house and roused three colleagues, James Timmins, James Partridge and John Higginson. The first two went to old Joe's shack with him, but Higginson refused on the basis that he had seen a friend burned in a boiler explosion years before and couldn't bear to see such a sight again.

Superintendent Woollaston and PC McHarg were called, finding a spade, a shovel, two rakes and a hammer near the body. They soon arrested John Higginson, who proved to have bloodstains on his boots. An inquest was held at the Nag's Head in Church Lane. In those days Coroners' juries routinely viewed the body and several were nearly overcome by the state of Joe Marshall's remains.

The Coroner only took evidence of identification. Isaac Blocksidge said that he knew Marshall well, that he was about 50 years old, a good age for a working man in those days, and that he had last seen him alive at about 8.00 on Saturday night in the Nag's Head. The Coroner then

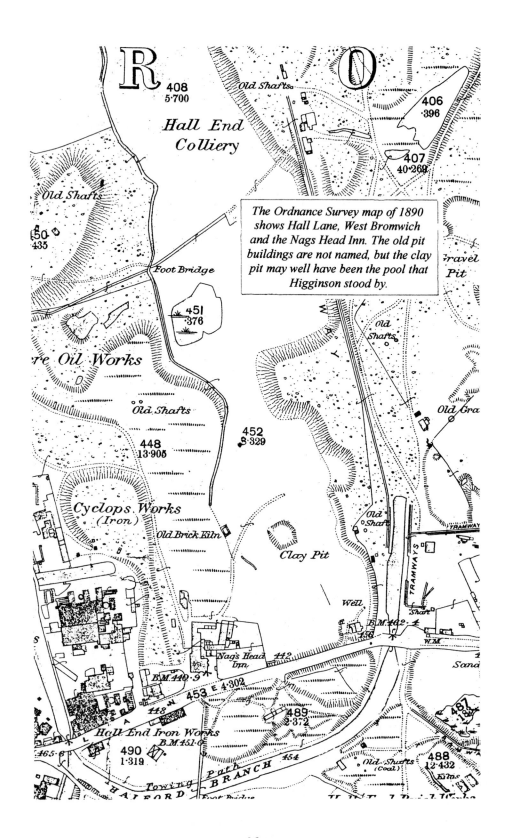

The Ordnance Survey map of 1890 shows Hall Lane, West Bromwich and the Nags Head Inn. The old pit buildings are not named, but the clay pit may well have been the pool that Higginson stood by.

adjourned the Inquest for reasons he was unwilling to explain, nor would the police give the press any further information. Higginson was committed for trial at Stafford Assize.

Dr Kite of West Bromwich gave evidence that Marshall had died from the head injuries, his body then being badly burned by hot coals placed close to it.

Elijah Gurney, a stoker who lived near the Nag's Head, had seen Higginson and Marshall leave the Nag's Head together late on Saturday night, apparently arguing, and take the canal towpath towards the colliery. "Black Jack" Higginson, a huge and simple soul, had then left Marshall and gone to his home at Mrs McEvoy's lodging house which he shared with Timmins and Partridge.

At about 3 o'clock in the morning Higginson had got up, saying that he was going to look for mushrooms, but a witness named Moore saw him go to Lame Joe's hut and stay there about a quarter of an hour. "When he came out", said Moore, "he went down to the poolside by the pitbank and stood there for about 10 minutes and then crossed the meadow. I then saw no more of him."

Higginson's crime looked about as bad as it gets, unless the defence could show he was insane. This has always been a difficult defence because of the extreme standard of mental disturbance which the archaic law demands in cases of murder. However, the question of Higginson's mental state never entered the trial. The judge, Mr Justice Lush, directed the jury that the killing might not have been intentional, that it might have arisen as a continuation of the row the two men had been engaged in as they left the pub. The jury found Higginson guilty of the lesser crime of manslaughter for which the penalty was not hanging but imprisonment. Fifty two year old Black Jack was sentenced to life, though it was soon clear that he was not mentally competent and he spent many years in Powick Lunatic Asylum, near Worcester.

✱✱✱✱✱✱✱

What was it all about? The Judge's reduction of the charge to manslaughter makes no legal sense. That argument might have held water if the killing had occurred immediately after they returned from the Nag's Head, but nobody, even a simpleton, gets up at 3 o'clock in the morning and goes out to wake somebody up and carry on an argument. Jack Higginson must have gone to Marshall's shack intending to do the lame old man some harm, if not of killing him, and that was sufficient to make him guilty of murder. But why?

Joe Marshall had been made lame long before by a pit accident. He was also cross eyed. The crippled were always feared by 19th century miners if only because they were an uncomfortable reminder of what might happen in a moment to any industrial worker. Being cross eyed was worse. Superstition had it that cross eyed people had the power of putting the evil eye on others, that by looking at them they could cause misfortune. Some people still talk about evilly disposed persons "looking at you cross eyed".

Evidence at the trial showed that John Higginson was terrified of old Joe who had threatened to put the evil eye on him if Higginson did not keep him supplied with ale. He is said to have consulted a white witch who advised him that the only way to remove the curse was to burn the person who caused it. That would have been monstrously irresponsible and, in any case, seems unlikely to be true. The acknowledged way of removing the evil eye was to cause the person responsible to bleed above the eyebrows. It may be that Jack Higginson was advised to try that, and that Joe Marshall fought back and was killed in the struggle.

$$*******$$

The evil eye superstition was very much alive in the 1870s. In *Midland Murders & Mysteries* I mentioned a case at Warwick Assize a few years after Higginson's trial in which a man killed a woman with a pitchfork. He also believed that he had been a victim of the evil eye. The Judge spoke about the barbaric beliefs of rural Warwickshire and found the man insane. Perhaps Justice Lush thought Higginson insane and decided to save his life by inventing an excuse to reduce the charge.

If the Warwick judge thought the ways of rural Warwickshire uncivilised, what can we make of the same belief leading to murder in the industrial landscape of the Black Country, surrounded by foundries, collieries, an oil works and a canal? Essentially, these industrial workers were the same people a generation or two on, John Higginson started life as a farm worker. Cheap printing and popular education had done nothing to stamp out ancient pagan beliefs.

Nor have television, radio, movies, universal free education or the internet. Do you avoid walking under ladders? Do you know anyone who rubs a charm before filling in their lottery numbers? Do you sprinkle salt over your left shoulder if you spill it? I'm sure many of you do.

A few years ago I arrived at the Birmingham centre where I lectured an evening class on the paranormal to find an anxious lady from some nearby flats waiting to see me. She believed that a neighbour was putting the evil eye on her, and wanted my advice. I did not advise her to burn her neighbour, nor to try and draw blood. I fought fire with fire and gave her a traditional charm to protect herself. It seems to have worked because I never saw her again.

You can read further details about this case in *Accident, Manslaughter or Murder* by Anthony Hunt (published by QuercuS, 2001), which contains an absorbing description of the trial taken from reports in the *Wolverhampton Chronicle*.

"A damned sight better"
(Quarry Bank, Staffs, 1906)

Workhouses have been gone for more than half a century and what little we know of them probably derives from Dickens's *Oliver Twist*. We have an idea that they were grim places where the elderly poor withered and poor children were bullied by tyrannous and pompous parish officials while being fed a meagre diet of unappetising food.

All of which is true, but it isn't the whole story. Workhouses were first set up in Tudor times with the best of intentions, so that the sick, elderly or workless poor should not starve. They were administered by parish authorities and how good or bad they were depended on how good or bad the overseer and how much the parish was prepared to spend. It was never much, so most workhouses were horrible.

By the late 18th century the system was being overwhelmed in some parts of the country by unemployed agricultural labourers. At Speenhamland, near Newbury, the Berkshire Justices organised a new system which they thought would be cheaper and more effective. They would encourage employers to take on workers by subsidising the wages instead of having people doing nothing and being a total charge on the parish rates. Again, a well intentioned idea, and again it didn't work. Even so, it was reintroduced in the 1980s as Family Support and still exists in slightly modified form as Family Tax Credit. The tax payer still subsidises employers' low wages.

In the 1830s the Speenhamland System had driven farm wages down and down as greedy employers let their neighbours subsidise their wage bill. Farm labourers rioted across the south of England and parish ratepayers muttered.

In 1834 a new Poor Law was passed abolishing out relief, or payments to people not living in the workhouse. So ended the Speenhamland System. The Act was also intended to make the workhouse "as disagreeable as was consistent with health". Apart from brutal regimes, drab uniforms, insanitary conditions and bad food, husbands and wives were separated. This gave rise many years later to Albert Chevalier's sad song *My Old Dutch* and G.R.Sims much parodied poem, *In the Workhouse, Christmas Day*. The new workhouses were those that Charles Dickens knew and they soon became as bad as the worst intentioned of their creators could have wished.

In one London workhouse in the 1840s, a child disappeared. He was thought to have absconded until, weeks later, the great soup kettle of the workhouse was cleaned and his bones and clothes were found at the bottom. Presumably, like Oliver, he wanted more, and in trying to get it had slipped in and was boiled daily in the ration served to his mates. When an inquest sat the workhouse master did not deign to be present. Sent for and questioned by Coroner Wakley, he sneered that it had not even been proved that it was any particular boy. "Tell me", asked Wakley, "how many paupers have you boiled to death?" The case gave rise to a street ballad which blamed the overseer for pushing the boy into the pot and it might be the origin of the expression "in the soup". .

The plans of those who framed the Poor Law of 1834 had obviously worked and the working class became desperate not to end their days in such a place. They would suffer any indignity and work for the lowest of wages rather than submit to the horrors of the workhouse.

✱✱✱✱✱✱✱

One such was Joseph Jones. As a boy he lived in Pensnett, Dudley and not far along the street lived Joe's grandfather whom the boy loved dearly. One day as he came home along the street he saw two uniformed men dragging his beloved grandpa from his home and bundling him into a carriage. The old man disappeared and was never seen again. He had been forced into the workhouse where he survived only four weeks.

Joseph Jones grew up to be a steel mill worker, marrying and moving to Quarry Bank. He was well liked and respected but his world was darkened when his young wife died giving birth to a daughter. When the girl was 18 in 1898, she married a young chainmaker, Edmund Clarke. Joseph cheerfully allowed the couple to share his house in Quarry Bank.

They lived a quietly contented life, Joe had an occasional drink and laid an occasional bet, Edmund played soccer on Saturdays and sang in the church choir on Sundays, as well as teaching Sunday school. So it went until in 1905 Joseph Jones lost his job.

104

Idleness did not suit Joseph. Soon the occasional drink became a regular habit and the occasional flutter became a regular plunge, and soon his meagre savings were gone. Edmund thought he could save the situation and offered to buy the house from his father in law. It worked, but only in the short term. The money followed Joseph's savings into the tills of local beerhouses and the pockets of streetcorner bookies. Soon he was penniless again.

Edmund now realised that drink was the major problem. He gave the old man money but tried to prevent him from buying drink, an interference that caused anger, abuse and threats.

On the dark wintry Saturday of 1st December 1906 Edmund Clarke came home from his football match at about 6.00 pm and lay full length on the sofa, dozing. Ethel went out to complete her shopping. Joseph was already out somewhere, probably getting drunk.

It was after 8 o'clock when Ethel Clarke brought her shopping home. Her screams roused the neighbours and when they crowded in, they understood her horror.

The little sitting room was literally dripping with blood. It dribbled down the walls, pooled on the floor, soaked into the furnishings and stained the tablecloth. In the midst of this nightmare lay her husband, still stretched on the sofa, but now with his head battered until the brain showed and his throat cut from ear to ear. Joseph Jones sat alongside in a chair.

As Ethel screamed mindlessly, old Joseph quietly stood up and stepped out of the door, walking the short distance to Brierley Hill Police Station. From there he was taken to Winson Green Prison, Birmingham while police took possession of the bloodstained poker and two open razors with which he had killed his son in law.

No one could explain the explosion of violence in Joseph's brain, perhaps a combination of a bitter childhood memory, the fears of his class and resentment at becoming a pensioner of his son in law. His trial at the March Assize at Stafford was short, ending with a sentence of death. In Stafford Gaol he spent his three clear Sundays before execution as a model prisoner, if quiet. Hangman Henry Pierrepoint recorded that Jones's last remark was, "This is a damned sight better than the workhouse".

"Nothing more than a beggar"
(Burslem, Staffs 1797)

Wood is a famous name in English pottery, long established in the trade. In 1782 when the industry was growing and firms around Stoke on Trent were expanding, John Wood bought himself a country house between Burslem and Tunstall. With the house was a large wooded estate which included Wood's pottery works, and also wooded paths past a watermill into Burslem.

Mrs Wood was not in good health, so the delights of the rural estate were usually enjoyed by John Wood and his daughter Maria. As father and daughter strolled the spacious grounds, Mrs Wood was being seen by a local practitioner, Doctor Hickman.

The expanding population of the area seems to have stretched the resources of Dr Hickman's practice so that he took on an assistant, Dr Thomas Milward Oliver. In time young Dr Oliver was assigned to see to the medical requirements of Mrs Wood and began visiting the house.

The handsome young man seems to have been a better doctor than Hickman, for he soon cured Mrs Wood. His visits to the house continued though, now to see Maria Wood who was seen strolling in the grounds with the doctor rather than her father.

Initially the Woods made Dr Oliver welcome, but things changed. Whether Oliver indicated a matrimonial interest in Maria or whether John Wood merely suspected it, there was a blazing row between potter and doctor which was seen and heard by witnesses. It ended with Dr Oliver being forbidden to pay any further attentions to Maria.

It was strange period socially. The Industrial Revolution had broken the old, simple social relationships between landowner, tenant and labourer, creating new and different classes. There were wealthy manufacturers with money but no aristocratic blood, craftsmen with skills but no money, farm labourers with no land, lawyers, doctors and professional men with education but no social standing. Apart from the labourers who simply got on with hiring out their muscles, everybody else was becoming very touchy about their place in society. John Wood must have seen his daughter's business as being to marry upwards into the aristocracy, not downwards into the emergent middle class. Dr Oliver may have been deeply in love with Maria, but he would also have seen the social advantage of marrying a wealthy manufacturer's daughter.

A bad situation can usually be made worse. The doctor and Maria continued to see each other in secret until the late summer of 1796 when they made a tryst to meet at the watermill. Whether they were unlucky or deliberately betrayed we do not know, but Maria's father surprised the pair at their meeting place.

This time the row between father and suitor escalated from hot words to blows. Worse still, Wood told the passionate doctor that his objection to him was social, that he was too poor to marry Maria and, "nothing more than a beggar".

Now Maria was kept under stricter discipline and there were no more clandestine trysts. Oliver, without his love and smarting under Wood's coarse taunt, was further angered by local rumours that he had tried to marry the girl for her father's money and had been sent packing. He became depressed and neglected his practice, spending his time studying only the comforting draughts supplied at the Turk's Head inn. There he made the acquaintance of Ralph Johnson and the two became friends.

Ralph Johnson's interest was in pistols and after an evening at the inn he and Dr Oliver would retire to Johnson's home and pass the time making bullets and practising with the guns.

Spending the following Christmas with her frustrated daughter and her choleric husband, it is no surprise that poor Mrs Wood fell ill again. What is surprising is that it was Dr Oliver who was called. Perhaps a sympathetic mother was trying to give her unhappy daughter a legitimate excuse to see her banned beau.

Perhaps with the passage of time young Oliver would have learned to live with his disappointment, whether of love or ambition, but the professional visit to the Woods seems to have stirred his smouldering passions to flame. Now he hung about the Turk's Head uttering threats against Wood.

✱✱✱✱✱✱✱

His friend Johnson still let Oliver play with his pistols and on Thursday 26th January 1797 they passed another evening moulding bullets. At the end Oliver asked if he might borrow both his friend's guns. Unbelievably, Johnson agreed.

Oliver afterwards said that he intended to commit suicide the next day, but that seems unlikely, though he did take a drug with him next morning when he presented himself at John Wood's front door.

He demanded to see Wood but was told that the potter was not yet up and that he should go to the accounts office and present his bill to Mr Bathman, the Chief Clerk. That must have set light to his already overheated resentment. Even so, he went to Mr Bathman and repeated that he had personal business with John Wood.

Wood was sent for and eventually arrived. Accounts differ, but Bathman said that as soon as Wood entered Oliver raised a pistol and shot the manufacturer in the chest. He was about to fire the second weapon when Bathman grabbed him.

Wood lay fatally injured on the floor, gasping, "Oh sir, you have killed me!"

"Yes", responded Oliver, "It's what I intended".

Oliver was held by Wood's staff while a doctor was called but Oliver offered them a free diagnosis. "It's no use", he said. "He will be dead in three hours and I too will not leave this room alive". After which he put something in his mouth.

He was wrong on both points. Wood lived until Monday morning and Oliver failed to poison himself. The dose he had taken was so great that he immediately vomited it up.

He was committed for trial at Stafford Assize where a medical colleague, Dr Parr, arranged for his defence. His plea of not guilty was supported by a claim that when Wood entered the office Oliver had taken him to task and Wood had made a sneering comment, which so provoked Oliver that he had fired the pistol.

His defence team saw that they were not making much headway on that tack and changed the plea in mid trial to insanity. Dr Oliver was not insane enough to meet the extreme standard of mental disturbance that this defence demands, so he was convicted and sentenced to hang. The loyal Dr Parr stayed with him from the death cell to the gallows and took Oliver's body home to his family at Stourbridge, Worcestershire.

All this cannot have done Dr Hickman's practice much good, but things got worse. The Doctor's wife was accidentally burned to death and the unlucky doctor took up his former assistant's alcoholic remedies and died a penniless drunk.

Ralph Johnson, on his deathbed and rather late, thought about his part in the affair and sent for Wood's son to beg forgiveness. He never thought, he said, that Oliver had any murderous intent. He was forgiven.

There is no surprise in finding a doctor condemned for murder, they appear with tiresome frequency, but Oliver is rather separated from his murderous colleagues by using a firearm. Usually doctors use poison.

"Well -- you know how it is."
(Stoneleigh, Warks 1969)

Amongst the various means of killing people, poison has a poor reputation. It has been called "the coward's weapon" and often a woman's method of murder. Certainly it became very popular in Victorian Britain for disposing of unwanted husbands, but many of the great poisoners were male, to mention only Doctor Palmer, Doctor Cream, Graham Young and Doctor Shipman.

The attractions of poisoning are that it sheds no blood and requires no violence. This is ideal for what you might call the squeamish killer, and it can often be mistaken for natural disease.

The 1960s were the decade of the "Permissive Society", in other words, when society slightly reduced the vast range of things it did not approve of. An old joke says that if you can remember the 60s you weren't really there because absolutely everybody was stoned on cannabis or high on LSD and jumping in and out of each other's beds. The 60s was not a time when you would have expected an unwanted spouse to be a problem.

Even so, there were many people who did not participate in these psychodelic and sexual delights but clung to more traditional values. They may have strayed from the path of marital fidelity but they did so covertly and with shame. If their dalliances led them to want freedom from an existing spouse, divorce was still relatively difficult, so the socially unliberated sometimes took up the traditional option of murder.

Beryl Walden was born on Lord Leigh's great Warwickshire estate of Stoneleigh Abbey. Her parents worked there but Beryl became a dressmaker for a Leamington Spa department store. Among the Walden's neighbours on the estate was a family called Waite who also worked for Lord Leigh, in fact Mr Waite not only worked for him but had served with him in Europe during World War II.

In October 1949 25 year old Beryl Walden married the Waite's son, Bill, who was four years her junior. At the time Bill was a serving soldier, so Beryl continued to live with her family until he was demobbed in 1952. The Army gave him an exemplary character.

Bill Waite returned to Stoneleigh where he had grown up and took a job as chauffeur and valet to Lord Leigh, who was pleased to have his old comrade's son in his service.

The Waites were at last able to begin their married life. They were not troubled by some of the issues which worried most newlyweds at that time. Both had secure jobs and Lord Leigh supplied a home on the estate at No 2, Laundry Flats. The estate dwellers have been described as "a kind of isolated village, a very close knit community, and very parochial".

If the Waites had marital problems in their early years, we do not know it. Beryl soon gave birth to a daughter and life seemed to flow on in relative calm. At least, it did until 1967, when a shorthand typist called Judith Regan joined the staff at the Stoneleigh Abbey estate office.

Judith Regan was an attractive 20 year old. By the beginning of 1968 she had fallen for Lord Leigh's tall, blue eyed, greying chauffeur and they started an affair. The affair blossomed, disguised by the chauffeur's excuses for being away from Stoneleigh, and after some six months the lovers discussed divorce and marriage. It was Waite's view that Beryl would never give him a divorce.

It was about this time that Beryl started to experience health problems, including loss of weight and appetite and bouts of vomitting. Her doctor treated her and sometimes her condition improved, but it would not disappear completely. By early 1969 her symptoms had worsened, she had numbness in her limbs and was weakening rapidly.

By March 1969 Beryl was in hospital. Various opinions were floated about the cause of her condition, but nobody could be sure. None of them suggested poisoning.

After a few weeks of treatment her condition had improved greatly so she was allowed home. Beryl hoped that she was getting better, but shortly after getting home the symptoms returned and grew worse.

Perhaps that is the point where poisoning should have been considered. A condition which gets worse in one place and improves in another often arises from an allergy or from accidental or deliberate poisoning. More rarely, it can arise as a psychosomatic response to a place which the sufferer dislikes. As it was, Beryl Waite's condition was still treated as a mysterious disease.

Her hopes of a return to health frustrated, Beryl became deeply depressed. She also began to suspect her husband of an affair with Judith Regan, though her remarks to a friend suggested that she believed it had begun while she was in hospital.

Judith Regan was a regular visitor to the Waite's home, helping the severely sick Beryl with household tasks, and eventually Beryl challenged her with having an affair with Bill Waite. Unsurprisingly, Judith denied it and continued to visit, but Beryl's suspicions deepened. Eventually came a day when Beryl packed her bags and wrote letters stating that she was leaving Bill.

Now at last was an opportunity for the guilty lovers to free themselves. Beryl was leaving her husband, opening the road to a legitimate solution. You might think that Waite and his mistress would have seized the opportunity with both hands, but instead Judith Regan argued Beryl into staying with her husband. The poisoning carried on.

The only reason for murdering Beryl was the perception that she would not give her husband a divorce. So, what prevented Waite and his lover from taking advantage of Beryl's decision to leave him? It is difficult to imagine the emotions and thoughts of a man who would persistently poison his wife of twenty years to pursue his desire for a woman a few years older than his own daughter. The only possible answer must be Waite's desire not to lose face in the close knit community of Stoneleigh Abbey by a divorce. To secure his standing in that little community, perhaps to safeguard his job and his home, Waite continued his murderous course.

On 6th September 1969 Beryl Waite was very ill, physically wasted and sometimes delirious. The doctor called twice that day, once leaving some medication. He was called back again when Bill Waite returned home and found his wife dead. The doctor found him shaken with sobbing. Where had Waite been while his wife died? Out with his mistress.

Now Beryl's doctor became unhappy about the cause of death and a post mortem was arranged. Waite was thunderstruck, saying, "I don't want her cut about!", but the examination went ahead and found arsenic in Beryl's stomach and intestines.

If you contemplate being as mindlessly cruel as Bill Waite, be warned, arsenic is not only easy to detect, it leaves a record of when it was administered. Arsenic in the bloodstream finds its way to the roots of the hair where it leaves traces in the growing strands. It can get onto the hair externally, from the atmosphere or from contaminated hands, but Beryl Waite had been a regular user of hair lacqeur. The arsenic had not got into her hair that way and, in any case, when it enters the hair from the blood, arsenic forms bands of a chemical compound that cannot be removed.

Home Office pathologist Derek Barrowcliff analysed those bands in Beryl's hair. Calculating from the known fact that hair grows on average at one centimetre in 28 days, Barrowcliff was able to show the pattern of poisoning. He made it clear that Beryl had been poisoned only at Stoneleigh and only when her husband was present. There were no bands when she was in hospital and none when Waite was away from home.

Lord Leigh and the Stoneleigh Abbey community were astounded by the police suspicion of Bill Waite. No one could believe that he had persistently given his wife arsenic and watched her terrible suffering. Even so, the scientific evidence pointed to Stoneleigh and police searched the estate for the source of the arsenic.

A small private home collects all manner of clutter, including medicines and chemicals that should have been thrown away years ago. On a large country estate where animals are kept, buildings and equipment have to be maintained and vermin kept at bay, it accumulates even more. The search turned up all sorts of chemical detritus, but it also found something curious in the Waite's home.

In the Waite's kitchen cabinet, close to where Bill prepared his wife's morning cup of tea when he was at home, they found a small plastic container which had once held travel pills. It was empty, but a greeny deposit clung to its top. Analysis revealed that this was a substance called

Paris Green, which is actually copper acetoarsenite. In a garage they found the pills that had been decanted from the container and hidden in the rafters was a screw of paper containing Paris Green.

Someone had evidently used the plastic pill container to transport small quantities of Paris Green into the Waite's kitchen, but it was not copper acetoarsenite that killed Beryl. While the poisoning may have begun with Paris Green, it changed to some other form of arsenic, for Paris Green is a strong green dye, which was not seen in Beryl's body.

Eventually the searchers found more arsenic at Stoneleigh, in a shed were two rusted cans of sodium arsenite. Paris Green is not easily soluble, but sodium arsenite is. Now it was completely clear that Beryl had been poisoned first with Paris Green, then with sodium arsenite, and had been finished off with a large dose of the latter. And the only person who held a key to the buildings where the pills and the Paris Green were found was Bill Waite.

Waite was arrested and charged, to the horror of the Stoneleigh Abbey folk, but his trial at Warwick exposed the story of his affair with Judith Regan. There was evidence of weekends in hotels at romantic places like Andover, Dumfries, Reading and Harrogate. They had discussed marriage and planned a honeymoon in Majorca.

Asked why he was out with Judith Regan on the night his wife lay dying, Waite said, "Well, you know how it is". Asked why he had not suggested a divorce he replied that his wife believed in keeping marriage going and he "could not wait twenty years".

He was convicted of what Mr Justice Wills rightly called "a heartless and cruel murder" and gaoled for life. Having killed not for a great love but out of a desire to keep a house and a job as Lord Stoneleigh's chauffeur. It is difficult to understand such a failure of imagination, particularly as it all happened in the swinging, sexually liberated, do as you please 1960s.

"I am far happier now that I have done it"
(Wirksworth, Derbyshire 1863)

The Victorians left behind a range of confusing and contradictory images. There were the huge libraries, town halls, museums and water works, decorative, dignified and virtuous public works. Then there were the reeking, smoky factories and pestilential slums surrounding them. Brightly uniformed soldiers (recruited from the same slums) marched down the street on their way to seize some other nation's land. Pretty children in sailor suits and long dresses played with hoops and balls; while unseen others had risen in the bitter dark of early morning to work in the mills. It was a vigorous, selfish, unequal age, driven by curiosity and profit. "Can we do it and will it make money?" They did do much of it and some people made a lot of money, not caring much about those who had worked to make it for them.

A more placid image has come down to us as well, the picture of Victorian middle class recreation in the home, the musical evening. Family and friends would gather in the drawing room with someone at the piano and maybe a couple of other instrumentalists. Recitations and instrumental pieces there would be, but top of the bill would be those decorously sentimental songs; *Home, Sweet Home, Throw Out the Lifeline, The Gypsy's Warning, A Boy's Best Friend,* and so on. Young men and women met at these orgies and used them to advance acquaintanceships to courtships, always in the utmost propriety. Their passions, no doubt, were entirely gentlemanly and ladylike and bound by the rigid codes of their class, but sometimes madness crept in.

Perhaps Bessie Goodwin should have listened to the gypsy's warning:

> Do not trust him, gentle maiden,
> Though his voice be low and sweet,
> Heed not him who kneels before thee,
> Gently pleading at thy feet.

Bessie was the daughter of Henry Goodwin who had been an officer in the Austrian cavalry and was described as "one of the finest amateur flautists in England". They had lived for some time in Chester where

Bessie's mother kept a school in which Bessie assisted. However, in 1859 at the age of about twenty she left home to keep house for her grandfather, Captain Goodwin, at Wigwell Grange, near Wirksworth in Derbyshire. Before leaving home she had visited her uncle, a doctor in Manchester, and there she met a young man called George Townley.

Bessie Goodwin has been described as "one of the jolliest, merriest lasses I ever met" and as a "handsome, high-spirited girl". George Victor Townley "in addition to well-developed musical gifts, had refined literary tastes, considerable acquirements as a linguist, and fascinating manners". Even so, he was the son of a Manchester merchant and dependant on his father before he had much money of his own. Apart from that problem the two might soon have married and the story would have ended very differently.

Bessie Goodwin and George Townley

Bessie and Gorge Townley grew extremely fond of each other and became engaged. Neither family would recognise the arrangement and the Goodwins applied pressure to have it broken off. There was separation and secret correspondence, then another meeting and their vow was renewed.

The situation might have drifted on until George's prospects improved or the families relented, but in 1863 a third character entered the story, a young clergymen who came to visit Bessie's grandfather. He soon became a favourite of the old man and soon afterwards a favourite of Bessie.

By now Bessie was in her mid twenties, no mean age for a Victorian girl, and here was a ready alternative to George Townley. Her grandfather's friend came from a good family, he had prospects and was evidently smitten by Bessie. He proposed, she accepted and on 14ᵗʰ August 1863 she wrote to George Townley asking to be released from their engagement.

How did that polished young man take her request? We know from his mother that he was desperately upset, but a day later he seems to have stiffened his upper lip and wrote to Bessie:

> "My dearest Bessie --- Dearest you will always be to me; to say that I am not terribly cut up would be a lie, but, at any rate, you know I am not the man to stand in your way...."

All very straightforward and decent. It did not seem unreasonable that he asked to see her one last time and said that he would travel by train from Derby on Tuesday or Wednesday. The next day, Monday, he wrote again to say that he had overlooked an obligation at Bolton, but could see Bessie on Thursday evening or Friday morning. "Anywhere between your house and Whatstandwell [the nearest station] would do". On Wednesday he wrote from Bolton saying that he would arrive by the 11.37 on Friday morning.

He was obviously most anxious to see her, but she was anxious not to see him and wrote on Wednesday to tell him:

> ".......not to come on any account. I leave here today and cannot tell when I shall or can be back again. I do not wish to see you if it can possibly be avoided, and indeed, there will be no chance now, so we had better end this state of suspense at once, and say 'Goodbye' without seeing each other. I feel sure I could not stand the meeting.

Her letter reached Townley's home at Hendham Vale while he was in Bolton. His mother opened it and telegraphed him immediately:

> "Letter from B. Come at once. Will meet you at the station. Will wait. Immediate."

The telegram sent Townley home but he did not stay there. That night he slept in Derby's Midland Hotel and on Friday 21st August he took a train to Whatstandwell. At about 5.40 pm he called at the Grange and asked for Bessie.

To avoid her grandfather seeing George, Bessie took him into the garden and there they spoke for half an hour. What passed between them we do not know, but it seems that she agreed to meet him again. He left and at about 6.45 she also left the house. She met George in Wigwell Lane and they were seen walking together there between 8 o'clock and 9. Here was the image of Victorian respectability, the handsome, heavily bearded young man strolling in the August evening with his pretty companion. This picture had another Victorian side, dark melodrama.

Reuben Conyer, a local farm labourer, was walking near the end of Mill Lane when he heard "a moaning noise". He ran towards the sound and found Bessie stumbling along the wall towards her home.

> "Her face and the front of her dress were covered with blood. She asked me to take her home, and said there was a gentleman down there had been murdering her".

Conyer helped the injured girl for about 20 yards, then saw Townley coming towards him.

> "I went towards him and asked who had been murdering Miss Goodwin. He said that he had stabbed her".

Together they carried Bessie a few more yards, while Townley called her "Poor Bessie" and said, "You should not have proved false to me". Soon they laid their burden down and Townley sent Conyer for help. Conyer returned with two brothers called Seeds and the four of them carried Bessie. She spoke only once, to say, "I am dying, I am dying".

Shortly after she did die and they laid her down while Townley kissed her and said, "Yes, she is dead. I have killed her".

They carried her to the gates of Wigwell Grange where they were met by Captain Goodwin and his housekeeper. No Victorian novelist or playwright would have written the dialogue that followed. Captain Goodwin asked,

"What's amiss? What have you there?"

"It is your granddaughter, Bessie, murdered", said one of the Seeds brothers.

"What nonsense are you talking? Who would murder my granddaughter?"

"I have done it", announced Townley.

"You? Who are you, sir?"

"My name is George Victor Townley".

"My God! My God! You murder my poor Bessie! You villain! What made you do it?"

"She has deceived me, and the woman who deceives me must die. I told her I should kill her. She knows my temper".

A constable was summoned and Townley calmly surrendered to him, saying,

> "I wish to give myself up for murdering the young lady". He handed over a bloodstained knife and remarked that, "I am far happier now that I have done it than I was before, and I trust she is".

George Townley stood trial at Derby Assizes in the following December. Witnesses told the story and there could be only one possible defence, insanity.

This is a difficult one because English criminal law requires its madmen to be very mad indeed. It is not enough for them to be raving mad most of the time. To show that they did not have the intention to kill or cause serious injury, a defendant must show that at the moment of committing the crime they did not understand the nature of their act or that it was wrong.

One helpful example is of a man who cuts off the head of his sleeping companion because he thinks it will be great fun to see him looking for it in the morning.

This ludicrous rule has no medical content. It was invented by a panel of judges after someone took a potshot at Queen Victoria, presumably driven by the fear that some deep dyed political scoundrel might assassinate the Queen and then gibber at a court until he was acquitted.

Some years earlier they had dealt much more robustly with the man who murdered Prime Minister Spencer Perceval in 1812, the only PM to have been assassinated in the House of Commons, or at all. He was certainly insane in the medical sense, but they hanged him anyway. *The Times* announced that, "The lunatic Bellingham who slew Mr Perceval will be tried on Friday and hanged on Monday next". So he was, and the Thunderer maintained its reputation for accuracy.

As the evidence emerged in court there was little doubt that Townley understood the nature of his act. He had been at pains to point out that he had killed Bessie, but was he sane under the rules? His mother gave evidence of his extreme agitation over Bessie's last letter, of how his limbs twitched and she gave him morphia to calm him. She also admitted that there was hereditary insanity on her side of the family. More impressively, Dr Forbes Winslow, one of the foremost mental specialists of the period, said that Townley's account of his beliefs was that "of a diseased intellect". His views were supported by a Dr Gisborne, but the specialists could only say that Townley was now medically insane. The jury had to direct its mind to the law's definition of insanity and Townley's state on the evening of 21st August.

At the time the law did not allow a defendant to give evidence in his own defence, or the jury might have heard Townley's views for themselves and realised how deeply disturbed he was. As it was the judge, Baron Martin, clarified the issue, telling them that if Townley knew what he was doing, that it was likely to cause death, and was against the law of God and man, then he was sane. It took them only five minutes to agree and find Townley guilty. Baron Martin sentenced him to hang.

[Until 1875 we had three courts of the same rank as the modern High Court, King's (or Queen's) Bench, Common Pleas and Exchequer, which in mediaeval times had dealt with tax cases. Judges of Exchequer were known as barons. Between 1873 and 1875 the old courts were merged into a single court but Exchequer judges kept their titles until the last one died.]

Although agreeing with the jury's (legally correct) verdict, the judge wrote to the Home Secretary the next day pointing out the views of Drs Winslow and Gisborne and enclosing his note of the trial, "with a view to a correct opinion being formed as to the propriety of execution".

Home Secretary Sir George Grey was not convinced by the doctors but passed the matter to the Commissioners in Lunacy. They took a statement from Townley in which he said:

> "I have done her no harm. She is better where she is than if she had lived. I believe there is a future state. I am waiting to go to her. I shall be too happy to join her. They set her against me. She was my property. I saw her, and took away what belonged to me; what else could I do? I think she in the same circumstances would have an equal right to do the same."

One might have thought that this showed Townley did not think his act was wrongful, but the Commissioners decided that he was legally sane.

The Commissioners' strange opinion reached the Home Office two days before the intended execution but it was overtaken by a statement from three Derbyshire Justices of the Peace certifying that Townley was "insane".

Grey now sent no less than four doctors, "medical gentlemen of much experience in cases of lunacy", to examine Townley in the Bethlehem Hospital. They said unanimously that, "George Victor Townley is of sound mind".

Beset by such a range of opinions, it would not have been surprising if Sir George had fallen back on his own view that the jury was right, but he commuted Townley's sentence to penal servitude for life, unleashing a press campaign of vilification and outrage that snarled on for weeks.

Townley had told the Commissioners that, although he believed in a future state, he had no religion. Sent to Pentonville, he sat silent in chapel when hymns were sung until 12th February 1865, when his neighbours noticed with astonishment that he was loudly singing *Abide with Me*. Service over, the convicts filed out and Townley took the opportunity to swallow dive from a balcony to the floor 25 feet below. He died instantly. From the meeting of the polished young man with musical and literary talents and the merry lass had come two pointless deaths.

.....and finally.....
(Burghill, Hereford 1926)

This book is the last in a series of three in which I have collected some of the more interesting and intriguing murders committed in the Midlands. With that in mind I will close the series with a crime which, though it actually happened, seems bizarrely like one the classics of detective fiction from the 1920s.

Burghill Court, Herefordshire, was a solid country mansion surrounded by lawns, shrubs and flowers. It was the home of two ladies, Miss Elinor Drinkwater Woodhouse and her sister, Martha Gordon Woodhouse.

In early September 1926 there were guests in the house. It was the kind of setting and cast of characters found so often in the country house mystery novels that flourished between the World Wars. There was even a loyal and long serving butler, Charles Houghton, who had served the sisters for twenty two years.

In that late summer of 1926, with the Coal Strike and the General Strike out of the way, it must have been very pleasant to occupy a house like Burghill Court, to have the income to staff and maintain it and to entertain friends at a houseparty.

There was only one fly in the ointment, Charles Houghton. For whatever reason the once faithful butler had taken to drink during the summer and become careless about his work. Whether in sudden irritation or after thoughtful consideration, his mistresses decided to dispense with his services.

They do not seem to have tried to find out the causes of Houghton's descent into drunkeness after twenty two years of sober service. Perhaps they did not think it was their business.

His sacking deeply shocked Houghton. For a senior domestic servant to be sacked for such a reason was to guarantee that he would never work again as a butler. He saw all of his carefully acquired professional credit disappearing, but he seems to have recognised the justice of his dismissal.

He did not plead for his job, he asked only for longer notice, saying that he deserved at least that. Perhaps because there were guests in their house, the sisters agreed to give him one week.

On 7th September some of the guests were playing croquet on the lawn at Burghill Court when they heard what sounded like a shot from the house, closely followed by another.

The cook was the first to trace the gunshot sounds to their source. She ran to her mistresses to find them both dying, shot in the head and neck at short range. They were dead in minutes.

Houghton was heard running up the stairs to his room and when the police arrived he was locked in. Breaking down the door, they found that he had tried to cut his throat.

Houghton's dismissal was obviously the reason for his attack on the Misses Woodhouse. What had caused his drinking was less clear. All the explanation he ever offered was when he was charged. He said, "Oh dear. It is a bad job. It is passion". Passion for whom or what he never said.

Within a month he appeared at Hereford Assize. He pleaded not guilty and his defence team tried to show that he was always of dull intellect, that he suffered from epilepsy and that he had received a severe head injury in his youth. As usual with insanity defences at the time, all this evidence was neutralised by the prison doctor who swore that while in custody Houghton had shown no signs of epilepsy or any other kind of mental disorder.

He was convicted and sentenced to hang.

It seems a shame that such an ideal setting for a Lord Peter Wimsey or Miss Marple mystery was only the scene of desperate impulse killings where it was always obvious that the butler did it.